# MINDFUL
*Dreaming*

# MINDFUL
# *Dreaming*

Harness the Power of Lucid Dreaming
for Happiness, Health, and
Positive Change

## CLARE R. JOHNSON, PhD

Conari Press

This edition first published in 2018 by Conari Press, an imprint of
Red Wheel/Weiser, LLC
With offices at:
65 Parker Street, Suite 7
Newburyport, MA 01950
*www.redwheelweiser.com*

ISBN: 978-1-57324-734-4

Library of Congress Cataloging-in-Publication Data available upon request.

Cover design by Jim Warner

Cover illustration The Ispot © Brain Stauffer

Printed in Canada

MAR

10  9  8  7  6  5  4  3  2  1

For Yasmin,
the biggest gift of my life

# Contents

# ONE

# What is Mindful Dreaming and how can it help us?

Today, many people are asking themselves: how can I become healthier and happier? Worldwide, we have developed so many aids to create positive moods and enhance our physical and mental well-being, from feel-good movies to fitness centers and spa breaks. Yet there's an entirely free, natural way to increase our personal health and happiness. It even saves time.

Because we do it while we're asleep.

We all dream every single night. Too often, dreams are dismissed as unimportant, or ignored. But your dreaming mind can become your best friend if you let it—a friend who wants to help you to live a happier, healthier life; a friend who is available to listen to your problems and dish out wise advice, even at 3 a.m.

These days there is a lot of buzz about mindfulness, where we focus our awareness on the present moment and become fully conscious of our thoughts, emotions, and experiences. This interest in mindfulness is wonderful, as it means more people are looking to wake up in their lives.

But what about the third of our lives we spend asleep?

Imagine how life would transform if we learned to be mindful in our dreams, too! Recalling dreams and working with them while awake is a huge step forward for mindful living, as it connects us with the deepest part of ourselves. Mindful Dreaming takes mindfulness a step further because we are not only engaging with our conscious experience; we are also engaging with our *unconscious*. This brings mindfulness into the third of our life that we spend sleeping. Why settle for being only two-thirds mindful, when there is so much benefit from being mindful to what is happening in our unconscious? Dream mindfulness is not even a chore. It is incredibly enriching and can propel us into profound healing experiences.

If somebody offered you a wellness experience where you could float blissfully in a luxury spa pool, go on wonderful adventures, fly through the sky with no fear of being hurt, and return feeling refreshed and pampered without missing even one minute of work, would you take it?

This wellness experience is available to all of us every night, no matter if we're rich or poor, because it's an experience we can create in our own bedroom while we sleep and dream. Dreams are one of the few things in the world that don't cost a penny. Dreaming belongs to everyone, and since we all do it every night anyway, nobody can argue that we are wasting time by choosing to experience dreams mindfully. On the contrary, we get much more out of life when we engage with our dreams, as they can help us on the emotional, physical, spiritual, and social levels.

Dreams are our hidden self; the other part of us that we need to get to know if we want to be truly mindful of who we are and why we are here. Dreams can help us to heal because they can improve our psychological state, release negative emotions, and enable us to take steps towards wholeness. Dreams can help us to create our own best life: to live out our full potential and be who we really want to be. Dreams are gifts. They can make us laugh out loud in our sleep, or wake up smiling. They can give us insight into problems and offer creative solutions. Science shows that dreaming is important for our mental health and well-being. Neuroscience and neurobiology show that dreaming consolidates memory and helps the learning process. Dreams can also integrate trauma and resolve emotional problems, as backed up by cognitive psychology and studies of posttraumatic stress disorder sufferers.

Working—and playing—with our dreams can help us to improve our lives. But what exactly *are* they? Before we start working with them, let's take a closer look at what dreams are.

## What are dreams?

Dreams are experiences, sensations, and emotions we have while we sleep. They usually involve a stream of vivid imagery. There are various historical, scientific, and psychological theories about what dreams are. In ancient Babylon, dreams were considered to be messages from the gods. Hippocrates believed that dreams could reveal cures for ill health. Modern theories of dreaming include Swiss psychiatrist Carl Jung's theory that dreams tap into a vast collective unconscious of shared human memory and German psychiatrist Fritz Perls's view that every part of the dream represents an aspect of the dreamer.

These modern theories emerged after 1900 when Sigmund Freud, the Austrian founder of psychoanalysis, popularized the idea that dreams are messages from our unconscious mind. Despite the subsequent expansion of the fields of psychoanalysis and dream psychology, some scientists persist in believing that dreams are entirely meaningless; nothing more than the result of the random firing of synapses in the brain. More enlightened scientists and psychologists see dreams as a valuable link with the unconscious mind, viewing them as a potential training ground for everything from enhancing creativity and resolving nightmares to improving sports skills and accelerating personal growth.

To keep things simple, let's consider it this way:

Dreams are inner movies.

Imagine a whole movie company that exists only for you. It has a vast array of props, costumes, and high-tech special effects.

Its directors, actors, and camera crew are sublimely talented and creative. The preferred acting style is wild improvization. All of the actors are there to illuminate *your* inner life. They do this on a nightly basis, in an erratic series of emotional snippets, hilarious skits, high drama, film noir, and occasionally horror.

Your brain records your nightly personal movie reel, but all too often it forgets most of it the second the alarm clock starts to beep. This is an enormous pity because those dedicated actors badly want to communicate with you. They want to capture your attention and show you how you really feel about yourself and your life. They want to help you to fulfill your enormous potential.

More to the point, those actors *are* you! You are the star of this movie. Even the minor actors represent different parts of you and your emotions, fears, and desires. Your dreams emerge from your unconscious mind. They reveal the state of your inner self or soul.

It's important to mention here that dreams can and do go beyond the personal level of the inner movie. Some dreams seem to tap into a collective concern or peek into the future. Other dreams reach a deeply spiritual level of awareness that transcends the minutiae of our daily life. Further on, we'll look at lucid dreams and what I call "soul dreams" in more detail. For now, it's enough to note that dreams are highly personal inner movies that emerge from our unconscious. Let's look at why getting intimate with our unconscious mind is so worthwhile.

### Why is it important to communicate with our unconscious?

Sigmund Freud believed that dreams are the royal road to the unconscious. Is traveling this royal road worth the effort? Why do we need to do this inner work? Here are six good reasons.

1. Our unconscious holds the key to our health and emotional wellness by showing us how we are really feeling and what we need to change in our lives. When we communicate with our unconscious, we make a leap in self-understanding and can access this huge healing potential.

2. Through working with unconscious imagery, we can heal from past trauma, improve health, relieve physical pain, and overcome fears and anxieties.

3. When there is an open flow of dialogue between our conscious and unconscious, we naturally become more mindful in all areas of our life.

4. Communicating with the unconscious can lead us to a more harmonious sexuality and higher self-esteem.

5. If we have suffered loss, our unconscious will signpost the way to healing from grief.

6. When we wake up to our unconscious, we wake up to our deeper, wiser self. We are able to unlock our deepest potential and create a happier, healthier life.

If these positive benefits aren't quite enough to convince you that it's good to be in touch with our unconscious, consider the downside of *not* communicating with it. When we are constantly running through life, never giving ourselves a moment to relax, when we are under pressure at work and at home, or when we are going through a difficult situation such as divorce, bereavement, or job loss, we become more and more stressed. In this state, we lose touch with our unconscious because we simply cannot tune in to the needs of our mind and body. Our usual reaction to stress is to keep on running, do everything faster, sleep less, and stop only when we are suddenly knocked out by a nasty virus. Why did we get that virus in the first place? Because we were overstressed.

There is a strong, scientifically acknowledged connection between stress and physical illness. In 2007, the *Observer* magazine of the Association for Psychological Science reviewed evidence that shows how stress causes deterioration throughout the body, from the gums to the heart, and makes us more vulnerable to cancer and other diseases. Research in the areas of neuroscience, psychology, medicine, and genetics shows that when we are stressed, our body experiences a fight or flight reaction that releases adrenaline, cortisol, and also norepinephrine, a hormone known to seal in memories of highly emotional or traumatic events by strengthening the connections between neurons at times of great stress. This means not only that bodily functions necessary for good health, such as digestion and immune function, slow down and become less effective when we are stressed, but also that we unconsciously build up and store emotionally difficult memories.

Dreams have the important function of releasing an overspill of too-strong emotions, a bit like a volcano rumbling and harmlessly belching smoke. Of course, from time to time our stress levels build so much that our dreams mirror a full volcanic eruption (imagine a spray of boiling lava!), and we wake up bathed in cold sweat after a horrible nightmare. But dreams cannot do all the stress-reducing work alone. We need to help them. When we develop a more harmonious relationship with our unconscious, we experience less stress and establish a more harmonious relationship with our physical health.

*When we communicate with our unconscious by working with our dreams, we continue the healthy work of processing and releasing stressful emotions such as fear, anxiety, and sadness, as well as traumatic memories.*

*The more we release these negative emotions, the healthier and happier we become because we are releasing stress from our mind and body.*

### How are dreams important for our mental health and well-being?

There are a large number of studies in fields such as neurobiology, cognitive psychology, and neuroscience that demonstrate just how important dreaming is for our mental health and well-being. In the 1980s, biophysics and physiology researcher Candace Pert, PhD, confirmed that there is a complex biochemical communication network between mind and body. Immune cells have receptors for neuropeptides, or the "molecules of emotion," which are released during every emotional state. If strong emotions are not adequately processed, they are stored at a cellular level. These surplus emotions rise to consciousness during dreaming, and Pert theorizes that if we do waking dreamwork, we can help to release them before they become damaging by creating illness in the body. Dreams help us to process our emotions, and dreamwork is good for our health!

Dreaming also enhances performance, consolidates memory, and helps us to hone skills. In 2010, Boston scientists at Beth Israel Deaconess Medical Center gave ninety-nine people a computer task in which they had to navigate a complex 3-D maze. Then they were asked either to take a nap or to engage in quiet activities while awake, before trying the task again. The results were striking. Those who had stayed awake showed no signs of improvement, even if they had thought about the maze during their activities. But the nappers who described *dreaming about the task* showed dramatic improvement: ten times more than that shown by those who didn't. Dreaming helps us to integrate new information in order to directly improve performance.

On the biological and neurological levels, it seems dreaming will help us even if we never remember a dream in our whole lives. But when we do recall our dreams, we bring to consciousness our own unique brand of creative thinking. In 1999, in the *Journal of Cognitive Neuroscience*, psychologist Robert Stickgold reported the findings of his study into the ability of the dreaming mind to make creative associations. Forty-four undergraduates were woken from rapid eye movement (REM) sleep and asked to identify different word pairs. In contrast to fully awake subjects, these sleepy students were faster at identifying weaker, less obvious word pairs. This indicates that the dreaming mind gravitates naturally to unexpected associations. Highly artistic people are known to associate creatively even when awake, but it's inspiring to know that when we are dreaming, we all think more creatively.

When we open the door to our dream images and stories, we open the door to an entire new world of creative and healing possibilities. By working with a combination of nighttime dreams, practical dreamwork as described in this book, and lucid dreaming (where we know that we are dreaming and can guide the dream if we want to), we can become more creative, resolve our worst nightmares, find solace in difficult life situations such as bereavement, and tap into what is happening in our physical body.

## My path into dreaming

You might be wondering how dreams became such a big part of my life. My earliest memory is of a dream I had when I was three years old. The dream was so vivid, colorful, and real, that afterwards it seemed to give itself a title: "Drowning in a Turquoise Swimming Pool." That dream marked the start of my fascination with dreaming. There was so much light and beauty in the dream, at first. I was loving playing in the water, until I felt myself sinking too deep and beginning to drown. Then I panicked. But in a flash of lucidity, I realized I had a choice: I could either stay in the dream and drown, or wake myself up.

I chose to wake up.

That childhood dream has become a metaphor for my life: at a relatively young age I began to ask myself, "Do I want to sleep through my life and be the victim of events, or do I want to WAKE UP and create my own best reality?" For many years now, I have become devoted to waking up by becoming mindfully present in every area of my life: not only in my waking life but also in my dreams.

As I grew up, my curiosity about dreams only increased, and I became a very frequent lucid dreamer. I have experienced many thousands of lucid dreams in my lifetime, and in 2007 I became the first person to earn a PhD on lucid dreaming as a creative writing tool. In international workshops and private sessions, I have so often seen the positive influence that dreams and waking dreamwork can have on those struggling to overcome trauma, heal relationships, deal with illness or bereavement, and cure recurrent nightmares.

My own dreams have long had a noticeably healing function, as if their deepest desire is to free me, teach me, help me to cope with loss, and transform illness into healing. Lucid dreaming has helped me to heal from fibroid tumors, overcome creative blocks to write my first novel, find the courage to take important life decisions, and recover from the trauma of the near-death of my baby daughter. I've become my own dream therapist: whenever I turn to my dreams for help, I receive it, and this has improved my life on every level. *Mindful Dreaming* shows how you can do the same.

### *What is Mindful Dreaming and how does it work?*

By connecting mindfully with our nighttime dreams, we open up the door to our unconscious. We attract everything in our life through the thoughts and images we keep in our mind. In dreams, we come face to face with our deepest unconscious images. Through working with our dreams, we can change our dream movie, and in doing so, we enable ourselves to transform on a deep level. When we transform, so do our lives. The core concept of Mindful Dreaming is very simple. It goes like this:

> *When we work with dreams to modify the "inner movie" of the dream, we can change deep unconscious patterns that have been preventing us from living life to the fullest. We learn to heal our life.*

The average person has around six dreams per night, which works out to more than two thousand dreams a year. That's two thousand opportunities every year to heal our life. How many years of life do we miss out on through not recalling our dreams? Based on the two hours a night we each spend in dream-rich REM sleep, scientists estimate that we spend nearly *six whole years* of our life dreaming. How many rich, enlivening experiences do we lose through forgetfulness? Isn't it time to wake up to this hidden part of ourselves?

Mindful Dreaming is about the pure pleasure of a good night's sleep, the joy of waking up to inspiring new dreams, and how when we use dreams as a compass to navigate through life, our life responds by becoming more harmonious, more exciting, and more vibrant.

And the best part?

Absolutely anybody can learn how to do it.

A friend of mine suffering from anxiety who was too frightened to travel by plane practiced boarding planes in her lucid dreams and within weeks she was able to fly without fear. A creatively blocked man on a weekend retreat I led had recurring nightmares of ships smashing against cliffs, and resolved this in five minutes by rewriting the ending of his dream so that the ships flew to safety. Six months later, he told me his creative block had dissolved that day and the nightmares had not returned. A woman I worked with was so shocked to see an X-ray of her blackened lungs in a dream that she gave up smoking the very next day. A lady who attended one of my workshops was being bullied in the workplace and had recurring nightmares of threatening men. When she imaginatively replayed the ending of her bad dream so that she faced up to the men, she finally felt empowered to stand up for herself at work.

Dreams are integral to healing on every level. Healing is any kind of positive change, from the improvement of a physical or mental state or the release of negative emotions to simply thinking happier thoughts. Healing is moving from a state of emotional or physical imbalance to balance and harmony; it is a step towards overall wellness and wholeness. Disturbing dream imagery can be transformed into healing imagery and then embraced as a new, healthy emotional pattern.

When we practice Mindful Dreaming, we unwrap a dream by considering its symbolic imagery, do imaginative therapeutic dreamwork to transform the inner movie of the dream, and integrate this therapeutic work to absorb the healing energy of the dream. When we allow our dreams to breathe and change through waking dreamwork, we can alter deep unconscious patterns and move forward into a happier way of being in the world. Once the work is done on the unconscious level—the level of dreams—we no longer manifest negative patterns in our conscious life, and we become happier.

If we pay mindful attention to them, dreams can heal our life. This is Mindful Dreaming.

## *What you'll find in this book*

*Mindful Dreaming* takes you step by step through the process of mindful sleeping, mindful dreaming, and therapeutic dreamwork. This is a highly practical book. You'll find core techniques for unwrapping the symbolic meaning of dreams and practical tips on how to have lucid dreams. There are nightmare solutions to help with bad dreams, healing visualizations to bring your most beautiful and powerful dream images into your body, and dream incubation exercises, where a specific dream is asked for.

The later chapters help you to understand certain types of dreams, such as sexual dreams and health dreams. There are dreamwork practices to ease specific life situations such as bereavement and trauma. You'll learn to go deeper into dreaming and work with soul dreams. Throughout the book you'll find many transformative Mindful Dreaming techniques that will help you to modify the inner movie of your dream in gentle and intuitive ways. I've also included practices for overall health, happiness, and well-being.

With this book, you'll discover:

◊ What dreams are and why they are so important
◊ How to improve your quality of sleep and wake up refreshed
◊ How to have lucid dreams where you can guide and shape the dream
◊ How dreams can help relieve stress and anxiety
◊ How to transform nightmares and heal from the past
◊ How to become your own dream therapist
◊ How to create your own best life—the life you would love to live

Dreams, especially when combined with waking dreamwork techniques like the ones in this book, can be transformational.

Once we reconnect with our dreams, we can work with them to increase our health and happiness. As more people learn to do this, the more healthy, happy people there will be in the world.

Every night, each of us has the opportunity to work with the powerful unconscious imagery of our dreams and learn how to heal our life.

Why not grasp it?

Of course, in order to open the door to dreams, we first need to remember them! Here are some tips for improving your dream recall from zero to frequent.

### How to recall your dreams

When I teach creativity classes, people sometimes tell me they can't remember a single dream. When I ask them if they might remember a childhood nightmare (these tend to stick in the mind), they can generally recall one, even if it is just a snippet or an emotion. In Western culture, dreams are still not given much importance and this usually starts in childhood, with well- meaning parents soothing their child after a nightmare by telling them, "That wasn't real—it was just a dream," and encouraging the child to forget the nightmare instead of talking about their fear and learning how to change their response to it. Over years and years, we become conditioned to dismiss dreams, and so we lose any habit we once had of remembering them.

But all that is easily changed. With some simple techniques, we can reconnect to our dreams and begin to remember them clearly. Dreams are like flowers that blossom under our attention, so when we let them know that we are genuinely interested in them, they will respond. After all, our dreams are a part of us. So if you feel frustrated that you never recall your dreams, or if you want to remember more dreams, try this program to reconnect you to them.

## PRACTICE #1

## THE DREAM RECALL PROGRAM

1. Jolting awake to a stressful alarm clock is the surest way to banish all dreams. Change your beeping alarm clock for one that plays your favorite gentle song . . . and that has a snooze function. Set the alarm a few minutes earlier than needed and take the entire song to remember your dreams. If the song is always the same one, this will create an automatic response so that when you hear the opening melody, your dream images will automatically resurface. This means that recalling your dreams will get progressively easier.

2. As soon as you wake up, without opening your eyes or changing your position, ask yourself, "What was I just doing? Who was I with?" to bring your last dream back into your mind. At first, you may recall only a vague impression or a feeling. Jot it down anyway (the next practice gives tips on how to keep a dream journal).

3. Create a dream recall mantra to repeat mentally before going to sleep and at various points during the day, "I easily remember my dreams."

4. Whenever you wake up in the night, think back to what you were just dreaming. If you can't remember, don't worry. Just repeat your dream recall mantra.

5. Anchor the dream in your memory by thinking about it from time to time as you go about your day. Really focus on the images and emotions of your dream and relive it in as much detail as you can.

6. Develop good sleep hygiene (see "Sleep well; dream well" on pages 17–18) so that you are getting enough restful sleep to be able to remember your dreams.

Hand in hand with improving your dream recall is the act of recording your dreams. Keeping a dream journal is the first and most basic form of dreamwork.

)———(

PRACTICE #2

## KEEP A DREAM JOURNAL

1. Find an unlined notebook to use as your dream journal. It's good to have unlined paper so that you can easily add drawings and sketches of your dream images. You may wish to use the right-hand page of your dream journal for dream descriptions and the left-hand side for sketches, reflections on the dream, and the results of any dreamwork you did with this dream (more on this later).

2. Keep your dream journal and pen by your bed and write down your dreams before you get up. Try to make your dream journal the first thing you reach for in the morning, and it will soon become a habit. Even if you think you haven't remembered any dreams, open your journal and start writing. It's astonishing how dreams can flood back into the mind when we put pen to paper in this creative early-morning state.

3. Write your dreams in the present tense and from a first-person perspective ("I am running along an orange rooftop...") because this draws you back into the scene and improves your recall. If you are pressed for time, write down dream titles only, as this will root the dreams in your memory; then come back later on to fill in the rest of the dreams. If you don't like writing, Dictaphones and apps that let you make a voice recording are also good ways to record your dreams.

4. Go through your dream journal before you go to sleep at night, underlining any imagery that jumps out at you, writing down insights, or creating a list of your common dream symbols or themes. This is a great way of priming yourself to recall your dreams the next morning. You'll start to really enjoy this moment of rereading your dreams; it allows you to make a conscious connection with your unconscious mind.

5. When you've finished looking over last night's dreams, put your journal aside and say to yourself firmly, "I will have vivid, beautiful dreams tonight, and I'll remember them when I wake up!" Then try the five-minute meditation at the end of this chapter to lead you into a relaxed, happy sleep.

)———(

## What is dreamwork?

Once you have remembered at least one dream, you're ready to start working with it. There are many ways of working with a dream. We can draw the dream, dance it, write it, explore its symbols, or imagine a new ending for it. We can simply think about it. Every time we think about a dream we had, we are shining the light of our conscious awareness onto something that has emerged from our unconscious mind. Every time we become aware of an image as we drop off to sleep, or every time we realize we are dreaming, we are doing the same thing.

Try it now for yourself. If you can remember any dream at all from any moment in your life, bring it to mind. It might be a dream you had last night. It might be a childhood nightmare you can only half remember. It doesn't matter. Think of your dream. Replay the imagery, colors, and emotions in your mind.

That's it—you're doing dreamwork! It can be that simple.

When we shine a light on the dream by thinking about it, several things may happen. The dream might remind us of something else, in which case we can simply allow memories and impressions to flow through our mind. When we do this, we may experience a sudden insight, or find ourselves understanding the dream or our current life situation better. Or maybe none of this happens and we simply remain present to the dream. We are still doing important work just by thinking about the dream: when we think about a dream, we open up a dialogue with our unconscious mind and allow it to express itself to us in its own symbolic, image-rich language. This builds a bridge between our inner and outer selves.

But before all of this important work can take place, it is essential that we make sure we get a good night's sleep.

## Sleep well; dream well

Why is getting a good night's sleep so important? Sleep plays an essential role in good mental and physical health and quality of life. When we don't get enough sleep night after night, week after week, our overall health worsens and we're more likely to develop chronic health issues. We're also more likely to become emotionally unstable and have a hard time making decisions and coping with change. Sleep balances hormones, supports a healthy immune system, and helps us to heal. We seriously need our sleep.

Dream loss can lead to depression: sleep specialist and clinical psychologist Dr. Rubin Naiman from the University of Arizona's Center for Integrative Medicine highlights the fact that many problems commonly attributed to sleep loss are in fact the result of us not getting enough dream-rich REM sleep. Naiman refers to this as "dream loss," and explains that it is an unrecognized public health hazard that can wreak havoc on our lives, since it has been shown to contribute to depression, dementia, and what Naiman calls "an erosion of spirituality." Naiman emphasizes the importance of restoring healthy dreaming so that dream loss is no longer a problem.

Dreaming is good for our health, but we have to have enough of it. We need to learn to sleep well in order to dream well and stay healthy and happy. We spend roughly a third of our lives asleep, so a seventy-five-year-old will have spent twenty-five whole years asleep! It makes sense to make those years relaxing, fulfilling ones. The way to do this is by ensuring we have good "sleep hygiene." Sleep hygiene refers to the good habits we need to cultivate in order to enjoy quality nighttime sleep and full alertness during the day.

## What kind of sleeper are you?

Below are just some of the questions you may want to ask yourself to identify the kind of sleeper/dreamer you are, as compared to the kind of sleeper/dreamer you would like to be. Go through the questions writing quick answers. Then go through again, this time writing your *ideal* answers. This will give you a clear idea of how far you are from getting an optimal night's sleep.

◊ How many hours sleep do you get each night?
◊ What are your pre-sleep habits? (Do you drink alcohol or an after-dinner espresso in the evenings? Do you read on your iPad or phone right before you go to sleep?)
◊ Do you lie awake thinking (or stressing) before you fall asleep, or do you fall asleep easily?
◊ Do you wake up in the night and have trouble getting back to sleep again?
◊ How do you feel when you wake up in the morning? Rested and glad to start the day, or exhausted and moody?
◊ Do you often feel sleepy during the day?
◊ What about your dreams—do you remember any? Are they happy dreams, or filled with tension and conflict?
◊ How would you rate the overall quality of your sleep on a scale from one to ten?

If two or more of your answers are very different from your ideal answers, you'll probably want to work on improving your sleep hygiene, or sleeping habits. Keeping a sleep diary helps to pinpoint your personal sleep habits.

## PRACTICE #3

### KEEP A ONE-WEEK SLEEP DIARY

If you're not sure about the quality of your sleep, try keeping a sleep diary for a week. Every day, complete these ten statements according to your own experience, and by the end of the week, you should be able to see a clear pattern.

1. In the fifteen minutes before I turned out the light, I meditated/ worked on my laptop/read a book.
2. It took me around X minutes to fall asleep.
3. I spent a total of X minutes/hours awake during the night.
4. My sleep was restful/fitful/I barely slept.
5. On a scale of one to ten, I'd grade this night of sleep as X.
6. I remembered X (number of) dreams.
7. My dreams were beautiful/uneasy/I had a nightmare.
8. When I woke up, I felt good/exhausted/like I wasn't ready to wake up.
9. Today, my overall mood and energy levels can be described as X.
10. My further observations about this night of sleep are X.

Look at any connections that come up, such as late-night TV and bad dreams, or overdoing the wine and waking up in a lousy mood. If you find you're falling asleep easily, sleeping restfully each night, and waking up from wonderful dreams to begin the day with a sense of purpose, then you're all set! If not, there are plenty of easy ways to improve your overall sleep experience. Here they are:

## PRACTICE #4

# THE FIVE-STEP PROGRAM TO A GOOD NIGHT'S SLEEP

1. **Don't overindulge too close to bedtime.** We've all done it: opened a bottle of wine and had a large, late evening meal before slumping in front of the TV and then flopping into bed. But sleep hygiene researchers say it's better to avoid large meals, alcohol, nicotine, and caffeine close to bedtime.

2. **Follow the "only sex and sleeping" rule.** Using your bedroom only for sleep and sex is a good way of promoting sound sleep. Dim the lights in the half hour before you sleep rather than watching TV or surfing the net, as lit screens activate the brain. To strengthen the association "bed = sleep," some experts even advise against reading a book in bed (personally, I'm not giving that one up!).

3. **If you wake up in the night with a racing mind, sit in darkness.** One thing that often happens to me when I'm working intensively is that I'll wake up in the night and can't get back to sleep for ages as my mind is racing with thoughts. For me, this can actually be a helpful time for creative thinking, but if all you're doing during those wide-awake night hours is worrying about life or refining your "to do" list, try getting out of bed and sitting in darkness until your thoughts calm down and you're ready to sleep again.

4. **Stay fit.** Exercizing during the day promotes restful sleep if it's not done too close to bedtime. Everyone differs a little on how late into the evening they can play a sport without it affecting their sleep, so experiment and see what works best for you.

5. **Stay on schedule.** Maintain a regular sleep schedule and don't let it vary too much, so that your body is clear about when it's expected to sleep. Make sure you get enough exposure to natural light during the daytime, as this helps your body to distinguish between day and night and settle into a natural, beneficial sleep rhythm. Most healthy adults need seven to nine hours of sleep a night, but this varies among individuals. Afternoon naps can interfere with your nighttime sleep rhythm—though they're great for lucid dreaming!

>————<

Making adjustments to these physical elements of sleep hygiene can greatly improve your quality of sleep, and when that happens, you'll find that you automatically have more time for your dreams. You'll be less tired, less stressed, and the entire sleep experience will become a true pleasure as your dreams reach out to greet you. It is also really beneficial to create your own personal sleep hygiene ritual and use it every night to ease you into a delightful night of sleep.

## PRACTICE #5

### CREATE A SLEEP HYGIENE RITUAL

1. Think of your night of sleep as a mini-holiday. You are about to indulge in overnight therapy at a place of great healing and beauty—what a treat!

2. Prepare yourself for this nightly treat by turning your bedroom into a peaceful, inviting sleeping space, and keeping it cool: studies show that keeping your head cool helps you to sleep better. Make sure your mattress and pillows are comfortable. If your bedroom gets light too early, use black-out blinds or a

sleep mask. If you are disturbed by noise, use ear plugs or a white noise machine.

3. Create a soothing bedtime ritual. You can do this any way you choose, but here's my favorite routine: a) Have a warm bath. b) Put on relaxing music. c) Use low lighting or warm-colored light bulbs. d) Put a few drops of essential oil on your pillow: lavender and chamomile are good for promoting sleep. e) Meditate for five to ten minutes to clear your mind and help you to relax and wind down. At the end of this chapter is a very simple meditation that works well right before bed.

4. Once your bedtime ritual is established and you feel that you are sleeping better, you can set an intention to remember your dreams by saying to yourself before you sleep, "I will wake up refreshed and remember my dreams." When you wake up in the morning, remember and record your dreams, and before you get out of bed, think of at least one thing you're grateful for. It might simply be the fact that you have remembered a dream! Smile. It makes for a great start to the day.

)————(

Sleep is important; not least because when we sleep well, we dream well. Good sleep hygiene is a stepping stone into the wonderfully relaxing lifestyle practice of Mindful Dreaming.

I invite you to dream yourself well!

## PRACTICE #6

# A FIVE-MINUTE MEDITATION BEFORE BED

1. Sit up in bed; close your eyes; and take deep, slow, calming breaths.

2. As you breathe in and out, choose some words to go with each breath. For example, you might breathe in thinking, "I am . . ." and breathe out thinking, ". . . peaceful." This is called a mantra, and it will help you to stay focused on your breath and to relax more deeply.

3. In the gaps between thoughts, you'll float for a moment in peaceful space. These are the golden moments in meditation, and the idea is to relax and allow these moments to extend effortlessly so that you enter a state of great stillness and peace. The more often you meditate, the more golden moments you'll experience, and the longer they'll become. Just let them arise without striving for them.

4. Thoughts will involuntarily arise while you meditate, because your brain is naturally busy and inventive and wants to grab your attention. Don't worry about this. Every time new thoughts creep in, notice them without engaging with them or judging them. Use them as a reminder to return your awareness to your breath and repeat your mantra.

5. Do this meditation for as long as you want to, accepting the gentle rhythm of mantra . . . relaxation . . . thoughts . . . mantra . . . relaxation . . . thoughts.

6. As you settle into your pillow and close your eyes, try smiling—a genuine smile—and saying to yourself, "Tonight I will sleep and dream well."

)———(

TWO

# Understanding dreams
## *core techniques*

The saying goes that "eyes are the window to the soul." The same thing can be said of dreams. Dreams reveal to us the state of our soul; they mirror our feelings and preoccupations by painting a cinematic picture of how we are experiencing life at that moment. Dreams don't lie. They are not concerned with pulling the wool over our eyes and going along with our preferred version of the truth. Dreams are honest mirrors. We just need to work out what they are reflecting. An ancient Jewish proverb says, "An unexamined dream is like an unopened letter." Although our emotional response to a dream may be immediate and obvious, until we work with a dream and unravel its symbolic imagery, its deeper message may be lost to us. Dreams speak in a fabulous mixture of images, metaphors, and emotions that can be felt in the body. Have you ever woken up in the morning feeling sad, anxious, or insecure? Chances are you had a bad dream. And maybe you sometimes wake up laughing, or feeling unimaginably good? Dreams can powerfully influence our waking moods.

There is only one universal language in the world, and that's the language of dreams. When we understand dream symbolism, we open the door to our inner life. All over the world, dreams express themselves in rich, emotional imagery. This imagery may differ due to cultural context, but the symbolic meaning is conveyed in the same way. A child from a remote village in India might dream that mangoes rain down from heaven. While an American child's dream might replace the heaven-sent mangoes with pizza slices, the same sense would remain: that of gifts raining down from an abundant universe. We all started dreaming inside our mother's womb, and we will continue to dream for our whole life. This dream link we have with every other human being on the planet is a truly beautiful thing.

The universal language of dreams transcends all of the barriers we erect between ourselves and others. No matter our religious beliefs, cultural heritage, skin color, gender, sexual orientation, age, or mother tongue, we all dream every single night. Dreams around the globe reflect universal themes, joys, and sorrows. If we learn just one other language in our lifetime, let it be the language of dreams!

This chapter shows how to decipher the symbolic language of dreams, to give you an idea of how images can reflect specific feelings, events, and attitudes. We'll look at five different types of dreams and you'll learn core dreamwork techniques for understanding your dreams.

### Cracking the code: how to understand the symbolic language of dreams

We use metaphoric, symbolic language all the time in daily life. Every culture has its own collection of wise sayings, or idioms, which paint a picture of a situation: she has too many eggs in one basket; he let the cat out of the bag; every cloud has a silver lining; she got a taste of her own medicine; he's missed the boat; we'll cross that bridge when we come to it. Dreams love this picture-language and it is one of their preferred ways of communicating with us.

But when we first look at a dream, it can seem completely mystifying. It's actually good to approach the dream from a standpoint of not-knowing. This keeps us on our toes. It helps us to be flexible and open to the dream's possible meaning. When we slap an instant interpretation onto a dream and cling stubbornly to this interpretation, we risk suffocating the dream. Dreams need to breathe, just as we do. This is why dreamwork is a process: there are often questions to be asked; associations to be made. The dream can be unwrapped, revealing its heart as we peel back the layers.

Getting to know the language of dreams is so exciting. It's exhilarating to crack the code of a dream that's been troubling you and experience that rush of recognition that dream therapists call the "Aha" moment. If you're tempted to rush out and buy a dream dictionary, remember that although they can offer interesting perspectives, many give a simplistic, blanket meaning for each image. Yet every dream image will have different associations for different dreamers, and it's vital to remain open to possible meanings. A cow will have a hugely different personal meaning for a butcher than for a Hindu, for whom cows are sacred animals. A broken kite will have a different association for someone whose daughter's kite broke the day before, than for someone who has just been sacked from a high-flying job. For this reason, I wouldn't recommend relying on a dream dictionary too heavily for this process. Instead, I'll show you how to unlock the symbolic meaning of your own dreams in such a way that you gain insight into your specific life situation and your inner self.

To understand our dreams, we need to speak their dense symbolic language. How do we learn it?

In dream language, a tidal wave often relates to feelings of being overwhelmed, and a dream of taking an exam with no idea of the answers often connects to feeling unprepared in a waking life situation. A dream of being naked in public may relate to having revealed too much of ourselves. Only the dreamer can know the true meaning of their own dream, as associations are so personal, but familiarity with the language of dreams is key to understanding their possible meaning. The good news is that learning the language of dreams is much easier than you may think, and you'll quickly get the hang of it.

Sometimes it gives clarity to a dream to see which category (or categories) it falls into. Let's take a quick look at five different types of dream.

### Five types of dream

Dreams can be roughly divided into five categories: physical, emotional, archetypal, lucid, and soul dreams. Many dreams will contain elements of more than one of these categories.

### Physical dreams

These relate to your body: are you cold, hot, or exhausted? Do you need to pee? (We've all had those maddening dreams of hunting for a bathroom.) Are you ill or in pain? Physical sensations, pain, and illness that we are currently experiencing in our body can be woven into our inner movie in the form of unpleasant imagery, but if we manage to change any negative imagery while we're in the dream, this may help to relieve the pain. A friend of mine went to sleep with a headache that she'd had for two days. She dreamed she was wearing a tight metal band on her head. In the dream, she managed to take it off, and when she woke up, her headache was gone.

In a far more serious case, journalist Marc Barasch dreamed he was being tortured with hot coals beneath his chin, and it turned out he had thyroid cancer. Although dreams can sometimes forewarn illness, as seen in chapter 8, dreams of pain or violence do not necessarily indicate a physical problem in the body; most such dreams have psychological roots and tend to reflect an intense psychological experience or strong unresolved emotions. It's important to pay attention to such dreams and work with them to unwrap their deeper meaning. The main thing to recognize here is that some dreams do have their roots in physical sensations.

## Emotional dreams

We are bound to dream about what concerns us, frightens us, or makes us happy. Emotional dreams tend to have a psychological and personal focus. They involve clearly identifiable feelings such as sadness, happiness, loss, disbelief, surprise, horror, fear, and so on. For example, a friend of mine dreamed she was furiously smashing plate after plate in the kitchen while her husband watched helplessly. A woman I worked with dreamed she was crawling through a giant labyrinth made from cardboard boxes and couldn't see a way out. She was filled with panic at the thought of being trapped until she died. In such dreams, the setting and the action serve to illuminate the emotion that is hidden in our unconscious. The dream shows us how we *really* feel. When dream emotions are this extreme, they are calling out to be worked with, as shown in this chapter.

## Archetypal dreams

Dreams can contain archetypal symbols—universal images, characters, and themes that appear in all cultures throughout time in anything from legends and myths to cartoons and comic books. Archetypes are universally present in individual psyches. The "psyche" is the soul, mind, or spirit. Carl Jung believed that archetypes embody basic human experiences and universal meanings. They are the heart and soul of many of our favorite stories, from fairy tales to blockbuster movies: we all recognize the archetype of the Mentor (for example, Obi-Wan Kenobi in *Star Wars*) who trains the Hero for a quest, or the archetypal Old Hag (the witch in *Hansel and Gretel*), or the Trickster (Rumpelstiltskin). Archetypes can be both positive and negative, and they embody energies that are deeply familiar to us. In dreams they often transcend the mundane level of our waking life to reveal something deeper.

Look out for archetypal figures in your dreams, such as the Divine Child, the Healer, the Lover, the Martyr, the Judge, the Warrior, the Goddess, the Shape-shifter, and many others. If you're interested in learning more about archetypes, it might be an idea to find yourself a deck of archetype cards so that you can familiarize yourself with the positive and negative elements associated with each one. Thinking in terms of archetypes can be a useful way of shedding light on a dream that seems dense or hard to understand. Many dreams will have archetypal elements or characters, but truly archetypal dreams are highly symbolic dreams that tend to deal with core issues such as creation, death, crisis, and rebirth. Universal patterns of human nature can be seen, usually in the form of timeless images.

I once spoke at a conference where a man shared his dream of a towering cathedral. When he went inside, he saw a hole in the stone floor. Peering into it, he saw a red devil with a pitchfork. The dream places the universal figure of the devil in the heart of a symbol of Christian faith—the cathedral. Such a dream may reflect the emergence of a repressed or "shadow" aspect of the dreamer, or a spiritual crisis. The dream uses shock tactics and powerful religious archetypes to grab the dreamer's attention and cry, "Something's going on here that you need to know about!"

## Lucid dreams

These dreams may fall into any of the other categories shown here, but the difference is that lucid dreamers *know* that they are dreaming while they are dreaming. Lucid dreams are often especially vivid and memorable. The lucid dreamer can also guide the dream and choose to respond to the dream scenario in a particular way: to face a fear, for example, or to realize impossible fantasies, like flying to the stars. Chapter 3 explores lucid dreams further.

## Soul dreams

These are dreams of the higher; of spirit and soul. They often involve light, beautiful nature, or luminous beings, and have a spiritual quality. A woman I know dreamed of a glowing, energized female Buddha floating above her bed. I once dreamed of columns of blue light that seemed wise beyond belief. Such dreams connect us with a deep source of light and knowledge that we all have somewhere within. Chapter 10 explores soul dreams.

## *Some examples of dream interpretation*

The following are simplified examples of dream interpretation, to give you an idea of the way that dreams can communicate, and the importance of context and analysis in understanding them. Only the dreamer can truly know what his dream is about, and it's important to be respectful of this at all times: never impose your interpretation of somebody's dream onto them. *The dream belongs to the dreamer!*

*The radiator cap explodes off my car.*
Could this mean that the dreamer will have car trouble this week? Does it indicate that something is wrong in his body? This dream is a riddle until the dreamer tells us that he lost his temper badly the day before. Now it makes much more sense! We even have an idiom very close to this that expresses someone losing their temper, "He blew a gasket." This dream is likely to reflect the man processing his out-of-control behaviour from the previous day.

*I have to cross to the other side of the street.*
What an everyday dream this is, you might think. How mundane—he has to cross the street. Some people might say this is typical of the meaningless nonsense that dreams chuck at us in the night. But what if I were to tell you that the dreamer is a man

who is dying of AIDS? There's an expression commonly used in the US: "He crossed over to the other side." Now we see that there is nothing boring or everyday about the dream: this man is preparing himself for the ultimate journey we'll all take one day—the journey into death.

*A floating pair of magician's gloves dance in the air. Then they come close and start choking me.*
This dream has very unusual imagery: what on earth might it be about? Did the dreamer watch a horror film before bed? This dream is only understood when we learn that the dreamer is a little girl who has this dream whenever she becomes asthmatic. Her physical symptoms of not being able to breathe are translated by her dreaming mind into imagery of being choked.

*A dying dolphin is out of the water and is completely drying up.*
Why would anyone dream of a dying, drying-up dolphin? To discover more about the dream, we need to find out the dreamer's associations, life situation, and insights. This is why "the dream belongs to the dreamer": only the dreamer can really know what the dream is about. This dreamer was a blocked artist who felt that his creative inspiration (aka the dolphin) was completely drying up.

Dreams are deep, but they're indirect. This indirectness is exactly what can make them so opaque sometimes, even to their cocreator, the dreamer. Each of the dreams we've just looked at addresses deep issues and concerns, holding up a mirror to show the dreamer how he or she experiences life events. Yet none of these dreams is direct. All of them speak in metaphor. Were you able to see the symbolic ways in which these dreams communicate the truth of each situation? If so, you'll soon be conversing fluently with your unconscious.

Welcome to the symbolic, emotional language of dreams!

## *How to unwrap a dream: core techniques*

Dreams are like onions; their heart is hidden under many layers. Some dreams can be unwrapped over weeks, months, or even years, continuing to reveal rich new layers of meaning. Here are some quick and easy ways of reaching the heart of a dream.

### PRACTICE #7

### RE-ENTER THE DREAM

You'll find variations on this basic technique throughout the book, as it's an excellent way of beginning to work with a dream. Carl Jung developed a technique called "active imagination" to focus on any inner imagery, such as memories or daydreams, or even a mood or emotion, in order to discover more about it. In terms of dreams, active imagination means that a dreamer imaginatively re-enters a dream while awake.

1. Find a quiet space where you can relax and close your eyes.
2. Bring the memory of your dream vividly into your mind. See the colors, feel the emotions again, notice the details. Take a moment to conjure up the dream scene and relive it.
3. Now you are ready to engage with your dream; for example, by focusing on the imagery and watching it move and transform, or by trying any of the following practices.

)———(

PRACTICE #8

# MAKE A BRIDGE TO YOUR WAKING LIFE

1. Re-enter your dream as in the above practice. Then identify the strongest emotion in your dream. Is it determination, joy, panic, sorrow, disgust?
2. Ask yourself: is there any time in my life when I have felt the same emotion as in this dream? Each of the above examples of dream symbolism shows how closely dreams are tied to the dreamer's life. Context is important!
3. This practice can be great for cracking the code of a dream, as it connects the dream with a waking life situation or past event. If the situation is in the past, the dream may be pointing out that you still have strong feelings around it. If the dream is connected with a current situation, it will be useful to do further work on the dream to move it through any negative emotions and into possible solutions that you can then apply to your waking life.

)————(

For example, the woman I mentioned earlier who dreamed she was trapped in a cardboard-box labyrinth made a bridge to her waking life and found that she felt the same sensation of panic when she thought about being stuck in her dead-end job. In the dream, she had been scuttling through the labyrinth on all fours like a mouse. As we worked on her dream together, she realized that all she needed to do to find a way out of her dream labyrinth was to stand up so that she could see the way out! This helped her to understand that she needed to view her current job from a different perspective and that she would then see a way out of what had become an unbearable situation.

## PRACTICE #9

## THE "ALIEN FROM
## ANOTHER PLANET" TECHNIQUE

This technique can be done alone, in your imagination, or with a friend who is happy to help you out by pretending to be an alien (what are friends for?).

1. Retell your dream but pretend you are telling it to an alien from another planet.
2. The alien doesn't know what a window is, or what stealing is, or what chocolate tastes like. As you tell your dream, pause to explain the key images and actions. Doing this will reveal your personal understanding of the images and can prompt surprising insights.
3. Don't give your explanations much thought—it's better to say the very first thing that comes into your head when you think of the particular image you saw in your dream. Let's take the example of a door. One dreamer might say, "A door is something you can go through to get to somewhere new." A different dreamer might say, "A door is something that traps you inside when it's locked." Each description gives us insight into the dream image of the door and brings us closer to the symbolic meaning of the imagery.
4. Your explanations of the dream images may provoke a spontaneous connection to a waking life situation: "I'm feeling trapped in my relationship right now, as if I'm locked in!" If you get a major insight like this, it's time to move on to transformative dreamwork as described on pages 59–65.

)———(

## *Unwrapping my galloping stallion dream*

For clarity, I'll use a dream of my own to show how the following techniques can provide additional insight until the dream is fully unwrapped. These techniques have no particular order; they can be used separately or in combination. They appear here in the order in which I used them to work on my dream. A good rule of thumb is, if you feel one technique hasn't gotten you as far into unwrapping the dream as you'd like to go, pick another one to keep things rolling along. Here's my dream:

> *I am in a park and see a life-sized sculpture of a galloping stallion that is made entirely from frozen champagne! When I get up close to it, I can see thousands of tiny, trapped champagne bubbles.*

### PRACTICE #10

### FREE-ASSOCIATION

This Freudian technique can be helpful as it encourages us to think freely and fluidly when unwrapping the meaning of a dream.

1. Choose a person, symbol, object, place, or situation from your dream. Focus on core images and characters first.
2. In a relaxed state of mind, consider the associations, memories, and feelings that come up when you think about your chosen element. Jot down your associations as they surface. A useful way of doing this is to ask yourself, "What is X [insert words that describe the dream image] to me?" When I began to unwrap my dream of the frozen champagne sculpture of a galloping stallion, I asked myself, "What is a *galloping stallion* to

me?" I came up with "strong, powerful, energized." Doing the same for champagne, I came up with "fizzing, heady, potent." When these associations emerged, I realized that the dream was about power and energy, but I still didn't completely understand it—why was this power and energy frozen?

3. In some cases, free-association might be enough to help the dreamer understand exactly what the dream is about, but if this is not the case, your initial associations may need to be combined with other techniques such as the ones below, in order to crack the code of the dream. I continued to work with my dream using the following technique.

)————(

## PRACTICE #11

## EXPLORE THE DREAM AS PART OF YOURSELF

1. This exercise works with the idea that every aspect or image of the dream is a part of yourself. Take the central, core image or event of your dream and imagine that this is an aspect of yourself. Which aspect would it be?

2. Having a simple description of the core image is helpful here, as it builds a linguistic bridge to the dream symbol. Instead of asking myself directly, "Which aspect of me does the champagne stallion represent?" I asked myself, "What part of me is strong, powerful, energized, fizzing, heady, and potent?" An answer came immediately: the creative part of me.

3. Once you have an answer to the "which part of me" question, you can deepen the dreamwork by asking further questions to work out why this aspect of yourself is in that particular situation in the dream.

Identifying the frozen stallion as the creative part of myself brought me to the crux of this dream: why is the creative part of me frozen? When I asked myself this, I knew the answer immediately. I had been focusing on things I *had* to do: research deadlines I had to meet. But what I really wanted to do was continue to write my novel, *Breathing in Color*. New ideas were fizzing up inside me with increasing power and insistence, but could not yet be released onto the page. The dream was showing me that I was containing this surging creativity with considerable force—the dream image showed not just a frozen stallion, but one made of champagne! Think of the force with which champagne corks sometimes burst from bottles. My huge internal tension had created this dream.

Now let's look at an imaginative therapeutic technique that I used to transform the inner movie of my frozen stallion dream. This core dreamwork technique involves an even greater level of engagement with the dream and can be used with any dream. It's a great way of getting into a dream deeply and quickly.

PRACTICE #12

## THE DREAM TALK TECHNIQUE

In the early 1950s, Fritz Perls developed Gestalt therapy, where people "become" an element of their dream and speak with its voice. My Dream Talk technique combines elements of both Jung's active imagination (see Practice #7: "Re-enter the dream," page 33) and Perls's Gestalt therapy. This means that the dreamer re-enters a dream imaginatively and then speaks with the voice of a dream figure or asks specific questions to unwrap the dream's meaning. It can be used not only with dream figures but also with dream objects or environmental features such as a dream river. All you need is imagination and empathy. Your unconscious will do the rest.

The Dream Talk technique can bring insight to any kind of dream and is good for nightmares, as it can help the nightmare story to transform spontaneously into something healing or otherwise positive. However, if you choose to work on a nightmare and feel frightened or unsafe at any point during this exercise, remember you can easily stop the process by opening your eyes and taking a deep breath.

1. Relax and close your eyes. Vividly relive your dream in your mind's eye: see again the colors, sensations, and emotions. Watch your dream replaying like a movie, then move inside it.

2. Which part of your dream seems the most emotionally intense or surprising? In your imagination, move towards that part of your dream and focus on the dream figure (or object) you want to talk to. See them and feel their energy and mood.

3. Still with your eyes closed, communicate with them in your imagination by asking questions such as, "Do you have a message for me?" or "Why are you behaving this way in my dream?" Notice any changes in their expression or body language. Don't put words into their mouth; instead, leave pauses for them to respond. This way you are much more likely to get a meaningful response.

4. Know that you are free to use your imagination. The dream is not set in stone: it can develop and change into something else. You're not stuck with your original role: you can act in any way that feels right.

5. If you want to deepen the process, try becoming one of the dream figures or objects and speaking with its voice, from its perspective. Imaginatively step inside them and speak from the heart. Say anything you need to say. Do this with as many

elements of the dream that you feel you need to. Remember that the dream is you, so you are speaking to different parts of yourself. Allow your dream to speak! You may find yourself going back and forth as you speak first as the dream figure and then as yourself. This might sound confusing at first, but once you've re-entered your dream you should quickly get used to this imaginative dreamplay.

When I re-entered the dream in my imagination and spoke with the voice of the galloping stallion, he melted my heart with his desperation. "Get me out of here, I need to run! Please, free me or I'll die." Clearly, I needed to carry on writing the novel to release the enormous tension of not writing it. I asked him, "How do I free you?" I touched the frozen sculpture and the stallion transformed into a real horse and galloped away into green meadows.

6. Depending on what you want, you might wish to ask for a teaching or a healing gift from someone or something in your dream. Just ask the person (or animal, or object) in your dream, "Do you have a gift for me?" Wait and see what happens, allowing the imagery in your mind's eye to transform spontaneously.

7. When you are ready, return to normal waking consciousness by taking a deep breath and opening your eyes. See what has changed. Do you understand your dream better now? How do you feel? You might find it useful to write down what happened when you re-entered your dream, along with any new insights you have into your current life situation and how you might change it if need be.

My dreamwork with the frozen stallion prompted me to free the creative part of myself from its temporary bondage: despite "not having time" to write my novel, I sat down and wrote scene after scene of it. This galloping release of creative energy actually helped me to get through my research faster, with a clearer head.

Alongside these core techniques for unwrapping dreams, it's always useful to look through your dream journal on a regular basis and notice patterns, dream symbols, and recurring themes and emotions. Doing this will help you to become familiar with your personal dreamlife, and the more you work with your dreams, the easier it will be to understand them. Stay close to the specific imagery of your dream and follow your personal associations to encounter the heart of the dream. This approach keeps dreams alive and allows them to breathe, grow, and release insights.

There are so many ways of working with dreams, and it may take a little time before you discover which techniques you personally prefer. If you're not sure at first which technique to use, re-entering your dream imaginatively and answering the following key questions can help to tease open its meaning.

PRACTICE #13

## TEN KEY QUESTIONS
## FOR UNWRAPPING A DREAM

1. Who are you in this dream? (A younger self, an observer, an animal, a different person, or yourself as you are today?)
2. How do you feel in your dream? What are the strongest emotions?
3. Do these emotions resonate with any situation in your life, past or present?
4. What is the core image or scene in this dream? ("Core" means the central, most arresting, most energized or emotional image.)

5. What are your associations with this core image or scene? Note down key words or phrases.

6. If every dream figure and symbol represents a part of you, which part would the core image represent? Use your key words to make it easier to connect with the core image.

7. If you were to ask the most negative or scary part of your dream if it has a message for you, what might it say?

8. Is there any light or beauty in your dream? This might be moonlight on water or a vibrant animal or person. Close your eyes and focus on it. Ask it, "What do you want me to know?" It might respond, or change into something else.

9. What does the dream *want*? Consider the actions and emotions within it, along with any surprise events or unexpected feelings. Sometimes stepping back from your dream and viewing it as if it were a movie can help you to pinpoint what the dream is attempting to convey to you.

10. If you could go back into your dream and change the ending, what would happen?

)———(

# THREE

# How to have lucid dreams

In a lucid dream, we know that we are dreaming while we are dreaming. We "wake up" inside the dream by becoming consciously aware that *this is a dream*. Lucid dreams are not waking reveries. They happen when we are asleep. They are not regular dreams in which we blindly accept impossible scenarios such as, "I am hanging off the edge of a cliff and a griffin swoops towards me, its talons outstretched." When you think about it, why on earth don't we become lucid sooner when crazy things like this happen? Most of the time we accept the dream reality as absolute because it feels so real at the time, and it's only when we wake up in a fearful sweat that we realize there is no cliff, no griffin, and we are lying safely in bed.

In a lucid dream, we know that we are asleep in bed and that everything we can see, touch, feel, taste, and smell is in fact a dream. This is a marvellous realization! Often when we recognize that we are dreaming, the entire dream scene responds by growing sharper and clearer, the colors more vibrant, the sensations super real. The beauty of this is that we have no reason to be fearful of anything in the dream, as we will certainly wake up safely in our bed. We can also do impossible things, such as fly. Many people choose to fly when they first become lucid in a dream as the sensations are so delicious: euphoric and hypersensual, as if every pore of the skin is tingling as we skim through the air. Lucid dreaming can be erotically charged—many lucid dreams occur in REM sleep, and a hallmark of REM is that the genitals are naturally in a state of arousal. Other lucid dreamers do not experience a particular erotic charge, but rather a deep curiosity mingled with alert attention and the desire to explore the dream environment or guide the dream.

When we become fully aware that we're dreaming, we can guide and shape the dream if we want to, or observe the way that our thoughts and emotions impact upon the dream environment. We can also simply go with the flow of the dream: despite what many people think, being lucid in a dream does not mean we have to control it. I've had many wonderful, surprising lucid dreams where I made no attempt whatsoever to guide events, but simply went wherever the dream plot went.

## Signals from inner space

The pioneering English psychologist Dr. Keith Hearne first scientifically proved lucid dreaming in April 1975 at the University of Hull. In the sleep laboratory, an experienced lucid dreamer, Alan Worsley, was hooked up to brain-monitoring equipment, and when he became lucid in a dream he signalled to Hearne with sweeping left-right eye movements that showed up clearly on the polygraph machine. These were the first signals from "inner space," sent from inside a dream to the outside world.

At the time of Keith Hearne's discovery, lucid dreaming books were simultaneously hitting the market, such as Dr. Patricia Garfield's *Creative Dreaming* (1974) and Scott Sparrow's *Lucid Dreaming: Dawning of the Clear Light* (1976). Further confirmation of Hearne's findings came later from psychophysiologist Dr. Stephen LaBerge's independent research in the US, which was published in 1981. Since those early years, there have been hundreds of research studies in this field. Movies have been made on the subject, novels have been written exploring its sheer possibilities, and everyone from neuroscientists to philosophers have devoted years to the study of lucid dreaming.

Now, the world is getting more and more interested in how technology can help people to have lucid dreams. These days there are smartphone apps and lucid dream masks that flash colored lights when the dreamer enters REM sleep to trigger them into realizing they are dreaming. Scientists are developing effective lucidity triggers: in 2014, clinical psychologist Ursula Voss and her colleagues in Germany discovered that it is possible to trigger lucid dreaming in the sleep lab by applying an electrical current of around 40 hertz to the sleeper's brain when they enter REM sleep. A staggering 77 percent of subjects became lucid in this way, even though they had never experienced lucid dreaming before. However, no matter how keen you are to start lucid dreaming, this is not to be tried at home! On pages 52–56, I'll give you my best tips for how you can naturally become lucid in your dreams.

### The creative power of lucid dreaming

For centuries, a potent mixture of dream imagery and waking awareness has been the cause of scientific discoveries and creative breakthroughs. Mary Wollstonecraft Shelley based the horror story *Frankenstein* on a nightmare she had in 1816 about a man creating a zombie from discarded human body parts. In 1844, the inventor of the sewing machine, Elias Howe, was struggling to work out how the machine could hold a needle. He dreamed he was captured by savages who threatened to kill him if he didn't finish it. Then he noticed that the tips of the savages' spears had eye-shaped holes in them. He awoke knowing that to complete his invention he needed to put holes in the *tips* of the needles. Modern greats such as musician Sir Paul McCartney and author Stephen King have attributed creative breakthroughs to their dreams.

Scientific studies show that lucid dreaming encourages creativity. In a 2010 study by psychologists Tadas Stumbrys and Michael Daniels, subjects were encouraged to look for a guru figure in their lucid dreams and ask the guru for help in creative problem solving. The results demonstrated that lucid dreams can contribute to problem-solving when dealing with creative rather than logical tasks and that dream characters can provide plausible creative advice to the dreamer.

My doctoral research investigated how lucid dreaming can help artists and writers to become more creative. One of my artist case studies, Epic Dewfall, simply walked into art galleries as soon as he became lucid in a dream and stood in front of the image he admired most. Then he would wake himself up and sketch it. One fiction writer would use the "impossible" physical sensations he experienced in lucid dreams as inspiration for fantasy scenes, such as shooting into space at the speed of light. Lucid dream creativity has no limits.

This extraordinarily valuable creative process is available to everyone who takes the time to listen to their dreams. It can be summed up in a simple equation:

*Conscious awareness + Unconscious imagery = Transformation*

Any kind of waking dreamwork brings our conscious awareness together with our unconscious imagery. By practicing the techniques in this book, we learn different ways of deepening this communication, but we can also tap into our creativity directly, by waking up inside a dream. In a lucid dream, you are *conscious* inside your own *unconscious* mind, and this can lead to powerful *transformation* in the form of startling creativity, psychological insight, and deep healing. Here's a visualization to help you get lucid in your dreams.

## PRACTICE #14

## LUCID DREAM VISUALIZATION

1. Visualization is a powerful lucidity aid, and it can be done very quickly.

2. Every day when you have a spare minute (and this is as long as it needs to take), pick one of your own dreams, close your eyes, and re-enter it. Vividly imagine that you become lucid in it. Now imagine exactly how you change it, or what you do. Will you swim like a dolphin? Go for a ride on the winged dragon? Ask the shady man why he's following you again?

3. Daydream in this way whenever you can. If you're at work in an office and can't close your eyes, allow your eyes to go into soft-focus as you sit in front of the computer. It need only take sixty seconds. Or do the visualization while waiting in line for your sandwich.

4. Re-entering your dreams like this throughout the day is a wonderful way of reconnecting with your dreaming mind. It will simultaneously send the message to your unconscious that you are interested in deepening your relationship with it and that you want to become lucid in your dreams.

5. Do the visualization again last thing at night, in bed with closed eyes. Repeat to yourself as you fall asleep, "Tonight, I am lucid in my dreams!"

>————(

## *Nightmares, lucid dreaming, and healing*

Lucid dreaming can help us to heal nightmares. In 2006, Victor Spoormaker and Jan van den Bout created a pilot study to see if lucid dreaming can help with nightmares. Participants were told about the possibility of changing nightmares in lucid dreams and given practical mastery exercises in which they changed the nightmare story into something more positive while awake. Those who became lucid or used the mastery techniques had a significant reduction in nightmares compared to the control group. This indicates that not only is lucid dreaming important, but also the waking mental practice of changing the dream.

We get attached to our fears. We cling to them because they are what we know, but they attract difficult situations into our lives and ultimately make us unhappy. When we find the courage to face our fears in lucid dreams, we notice the difference in our waking lives. When we work closely with our dreams, we can incubate dreams where we face our deepest fears, or simply remember to do this the next time we become lucid.

Lucid dreaming also has huge healing potential. It gives us the opportunity to rehearse our responses (such as turning frightening images into more positive scenarios) in a highly realistic, multisensory environment. The effects can be beneficial and long lasting: recurring nightmares can be resolved within just one lucid dream. This is one of the reasons why the use of lucid dreaming in psychotherapy is on the increase. In a lucid dream, you can do therapeutic dreamwork while actually in the dream! Lucid dreaming can help us to heal our past, optimize our present, and create our best future. Nightmarish figures can be confronted with the dreamer secure in the knowledge that he or she will wake up safely in bed; we can release ourselves from deeply rooted negative psychological patterns; traumatic imagery can be transformed into healing imagery. In a lucid dream, you can ask for a healing experience as soon as you become lucid, as Michael did in the following dream.

## Michael's dream: Healed by the Archangel Gabriel

*I become lucid in an old bedroom. I fly out onto the street outside the house and shout out, "Zamran a Etharzi, Archangel Gabriel" (Appear in peace, Archangel Gabriel) directly to the dream . . . I come across this huge helipad-type platform in the sky with a huge staircase going up into the heavens. I land on the pad, look up to the top of the staircase, and see this HUGE winged being! Suddenly the scene is filled with intense light, like I'm staring into the sun, and I feel this overwhelming sense of catharsis and emotional release. This being towers above me, and unconditional love and acceptance flow down towards me, melting away baggage I simply wasn't consciously aware of.*

When I woke up after this lucid dream, I felt my inner wounds weeping and healing, yet a day or two afterwards I was reinvigorated and rejuvenated with a new contentment and freshness to life. The process of cathartic release can be quite intensive as one heals.

## Lucidity and awareness

Lucidity relates to the larger question of awareness. How can we wake up in our lives? When we learn to become more present in our waking life, we are more likely to discover how our thoughts can shape our reality. This gives us the power to change our future. When we cultivate an awareness of how our life unfolds moment by moment, we bring greater lucidity to our thought processes, behavioural patterns, and relationships. We begin to live consciously. And what about when we sleep and dream—why waste those years of our life? Lucid dreaming is a powerful tool to help us wake up and consciously create our lives. What happens when we heal our past and optimize our present? We automatically create a better future, because we are happier people in this present moment. This is reality creation. It's all about waking up—in dreams and in life—and being lucid NOW, choosing our thoughts and inner imaginings, affirming our worth. All the power lies in the present moment.

With our thoughts in the present moment, we create the future.

There's no need to be a lucid dreamer in order to benefit from this book, because *working with dreams while awake can mirror the experience of lucid dreaming* and have powerful results. But becoming lucid in a dream can be such a healing experience, and so delightful, that it's well worth trying. Lucid dreaming opens the door to mindful dreaming. If you want to increase your overall mindfulness, try meditating for five minutes every day, and build this time up gradually until it becomes a habit. The following short meditative practice, which need only take a minute, will help you to cement your intention to have a lucid dream.

### PRACTICE #15

## LUCID GRATITUDE MEDITATION

Center yourself by relaxing, closing your eyes, and breathing deeply a few times. Now set the intention to be ever more lucid in dreams and in waking life. Remind yourself, "I can recognize I'm dreaming any time. I have this ability, and I can draw on it whenever I want to." As you set this intention, feel gratitude, as if your wish has already been granted.

The gratitude makes you smile inside. Let the smile expand right up until the moment that you open your eyes. Keep this lucid inner smile with you as you go about your day, and your life.

## What can you do in lucid dreams?

In a lucid dream, the world is your oyster. You can do anything you want, but some fascinating research shows that what people choose to do while lucid in a dream can positively affect their waking performance when it comes to sports: physical skills can be improved by practicing them in a lucid dream. Doctoral research by Melanie Schädlich at the University of Heidelberg in Germany shows that athletes can practice anything from swimming strokes to kickboxing moves in lucid dreams and see an improvement in their actual physical skills when they wake up. Researchers hypothesize that neural pathways in the brain are strengthened when motor activities are practiced in the highly realistic 3-D environment of the lucid dream.

In 2010, German researchers Daniel Erlacher and Michael Schredl carried out a coin-tossing experiment: forty people had twenty attempts at tossing a ten-cent coin into a cup. Some of them were invited to practice this in a lucid dream that night. The following day, all forty participants had to repeat the coin-tossing. The ones who had practiced the task while lucid in a dream showed significant improvement. When we practice physical movements in lucid dreams, we shape our own neural pathways and can change our waking performance for the better. Here are seven more things you can do when you become lucid in a dream.

1. Experiment with sexual fantasies.
2. Solve relationship problems by asking the dream (or a person in your dream) for help.
3. Try something you can't do in waking life—fly to the moon or turn yourself into a dolphin.
4. If you are upset, ill, or suffering in some way, you can ask the dream for healing, or send healing energy to another person.

5. Help the grieving process by becoming lucid in dreams of deceased loved ones and communicating with them (see chapter 9).

6. Turn sleep paralysis experiences (where you can't move a muscle and may experience frightening sensations) into beautiful dreams (see chapter 7).

7. Experience feelings of oneness, bliss, and spiritual connection.

〉————〈

The sheer possibilities of lucid dreaming, along with the media attention it now gets—helped along by the success of Hollywood movie *Inception*—have caused global interest to skyrocket, and today more and more people are asking: how do I learn to wake up in my dreams? A study by psychologist N. Lapina and colleagues in 1998 showed that 92 percent of people can lucid dream after learning the key techniques. If you combine curiosity, willpower, and self-belief with core lucidity practices such as keeping a dream diary and increasing awareness in your daily life, you will wake up inside your dreams. Here's my preferred program for getting lucid.

PRACTICE #16

## THE NINE-STEP PROGRAM
## TO GETTING LUCID

This follows on from the five-step program to a good night's sleep and the sleep hygiene ritual from chapter 1: once you've set up good sleep hygiene, you're ready to start lucid dreaming. This program combines practices for increasing waking awareness with lucidity induction techniques. You'll get the best results if you dive right in and practice all of these techniques together—why not start tonight? Lucid dreaming is a way of waking up to ourselves, to our lives, and to a vaster awareness of our place in the cosmos. It can be pretty mind-blowing. Go into it with respect, courage, and curiosity and you will be well equipped to lucid dream your way to a happier life.

1. **Keep a dream journal.** This is the best way of making a deep and lasting connection with your dreaming mind and building a solid base for lucid dreaming (see pages 15–16 for tips). Through keeping a dream journal, you'll recognize your personal dream imagery and symbols. The more familiar you become with these, the easier it'll be to realize that you're dreaming. Becoming lucid in a dream is a simple act of *recognition*—"Aha, this is a dream!"

2. **Meditate.** Meditation is a great mindfulness technique and a way of waking up in life. It's also a wonderful way of getting lucid in our dreams: just five to ten minutes of meditation before you sleep can work wonders. I've been meditating and doing yoga for nearly twenty-five years and find that both of these practices trigger lucid dreams. Observe your mind calmly, without getting involved in its endless loops, fantasies, and obsessions. Like a circus monkey, it will do all it can to engage your attention. Relax and allow its chatter as if it's a TV show going on in the background. As you shift your attention to the present moment (focusing on the breath really helps), the volume of your mental chatter will decrease and you'll drop into the occasional gap of nothingness, where for a moment there will be no thoughts; only awareness. This is a brilliant practice for lucid dreaming.

   Meditation strengthens the connection with the unconscious, gives us mental clarity, and teaches us to focus on the present moment. We need all these skills to get and stay lucid in our dreams. The more awake we are in life, the more likely we are to wake up in our dreams, as we learn to become more lucid in all areas of conscious experience.

3. **Carry out reality checks.** Ask yourself at regular intervals throughout the day, "Am I dreaming?" Try asking this whenever you see yourself in a mirror or when you reread a bit of text—in dreams we often look different in mirrors, and when we try to reread words, they get all jumbled up. If there's a stranger in the mirror or the words you're reading begin to slide off the page, you can be sure you're dreaming. Try this simple one-minute reality check:

    a) Breathe in and out deeply, noticing everything your senses perceive: noises, scents, physical sensations.

    b) Become fully aware that you exist, here and now, as the world unfolds around you.

    c) Ask yourself, "Is this a dream?" Ask it in all seriousness, fully expecting to discover that this is indeed a dream! After all, how do you know you're awake?

    d) Play around with ideas of what you would do if this were in fact a dream. Would you zoom into the sky? Ask for help with a problem? Practice your karate kicks? This moment of focused reflection prepares you to wake up in your dreams.

4. **Watch presleep imagery.** The often bizarre imagery, sounds, or sensations we experience before we drop off to sleep are known as hypnagogia. This is the gateway to lucid dreaming. As you fall asleep, notice the way your body feels first heavy, then light. At first you may just see wiggly lines or star-like points of light, but after a time you'll see weird imagery flash up and then disappear, and then these brief predream images will stay for longer and begin to move and morph into other images. This is the very beginning of dreaming! If you can stay aware as the images change and shape-shift, reminding your-

self, "This is the start of dreaming," you can follow them into a three-dimensional dream space . . . and the lucid dream begins. Practice watching your presleep imagery every night, even if it's just for a few minutes.

5. **Identify your state of consciousness.** You can trigger lucidity in any state of consciousness by recognizing the differences between your usual waking state and the other states you find yourself in, such as deep relaxation, falling asleep, dreaming, sleep paralysis with bizarre hallucinations, waking up, daydreaming, and so on. We all experience so many states of consciousness in a 24-hour period. It seems curious that we usually divide our reality into only two states: awake and asleep. There is so much more to conscious experience than this black-and-white perspective, and it's fun to explore and discover what else there is.

6. **Cultivate body awareness.** This is an effective way of having more lucid dreams. Tune into your body right now. Is there any pain or discomfort? Any aches or twinges? Are you hungry; do you need to pee? Your body is rarely 100 percent comfortable when you're awake. Do a quick body scan several times a day, and you'll get used to doing it in your dreams, too: are you free from pain? Are you feeling as light as a feather? If the answer is yes, try floating up into the air. Whoa . . . it's working—you're dreaming this!

7. **Take afternoon naps.** When I was at university, partying late into the night and getting up early for lectures, by the time 4 p.m. came along, I was well overdue a nap. Taking afternoon naps became a cornerstone of my life, and my lucid dreaming frequency soared like never before, as did incidences of sleep paralysis, lucid hypnagogia, and Lucid Light experiences, where all dream imagery falls away and you float in light (see pages 175–180).

When we don't get quite enough sleep at night, our body needs to catch up on dreaming sleep, so when we finally take a nap, we go right into what is known as "REM-rebound": a light sleep filled with bizarre, vivid dreams. This is a magical state of consciousness for all would-be lucid dreamers. As the sleep is light, we get lucid more easily. As the dreams are weird, we're more likely to notice we are dreaming. If we prime ourselves to get lucid before the nap, by falling asleep repeating, "I am dreaming this," we are likely to suddenly realize that we are indeed dreaming this! If an afternoon nap is impossible for you, wake yourself up in the early hours of the morning, meditate, then return to bed determined to get lucid.

8. **Use the power of visualization.** Bring a lucid dream visualization like the one on page 47 into your bedtime routine. Visualizing yourself lucid in a dream sends a powerful message to your unconscious and will help you to wake up in your dreams.

9. **Try the "Wake up, Back To Bed" technique (WBTB).** This technique has a high success rate for lucid dreaming—a recent, as yet unpublished lab study led by Daniel Erlacher found that even in the sleep lab, 50 percent of participants manage to become lucid using the WBTB technique. Set your alarm for five hours into your night of sleep. This is to set up your brain chemistry because you will now have your deepest sleep behind you and will be ready to enter a dream-rich REM cycle when you sleep again. A refreshed, active brain, combined with a still-tired body, is conducive to lucid dreaming. When the alarm goes off, get up for 15–30 minutes, write down your dreams, and do some other dream-related activity like watching a lucid dream video on YouTube. Then go back to bed and visualize yourself becoming lucid in one of the dreams you just had. If you want to remain popular with your bed partner, it might be wise to sleep elsewhere when doing WBTB—or alternatively, why not try the technique together?

)———(

### *How to stay lucid in a dream*

Becoming lucid in a dream can be so exciting that many beginner lucid dreamers simply lose lucidity and wake up. Below, I've put together some simple techniques to help you to stay lucid in your dreams. These first appeared in my free ebook, *Lucid Dreaming Stories & Tips*, which can be downloaded from my website, *www.DeepLucidDreaming.com*. A mixture of lucidity stabilization techniques is always best, so experiment in the dream and find out which combination works best for you.

PRACTICE #17

## TIPS AND TRICKS FOR STAYING LUCID

1. Remain calm. The moment when you realize, "Wow, this is a dream!" can be so overwhelmingly exciting that inexperienced lucid dreamers often wake straight up. It's worth learning a brief yet effective relaxation technique that you can practice while awake. If you practice yoga, you'll be familiar with the way that breathing deeply, slowly, and consciously will instantly calm your mind. Once you've found the relaxation technique that works best for you, try it as soon as you realize you're dreaming. My favorite is simply taking a deep breath in while telling myself, "I am calm . . ." and then saying on the out-breath, ". . . and this is a dream."

2. Touch the dream. Reach out a hand and stroke the dream wall, or rub your own dream hands together. Move your dream body—walk through the dream scene, feeling your feet on the ground, pat your head, or spin around in a circle. In one lucid dream, I found myself in a beautiful patio garden. I hovered over some spiky dream grass and grazed it with the soles of my feet to feel it tickle my bare skin. Then I sniffed a poppy, which

smelled perfectly realistic. This kept me engaged with the dream environment and stabilized lucidity.

3. While you're dreaming, remind yourself often, "I am dreaming." If you aren't used to lucid dreaming, you may get so caught up in the dream action that you forget this is a dream.

4. Do some simple sums, like 2 + 3, or 7 x 7. This stimulates your brain and makes it easier to maintain awareness.

5. Every time you feel lucidity slipping—the dream scene growing blurry, or sparser and less colorful, or wobbling like jelly—demand clarity. Say aloud, "Lucidity now!" or "Everything in this dream is crystal clear." As you say this, expect and believe that the dream will gain clarity in response, and it very likely will.

)———————(

## What if I can't become lucid in a dream?

If at first you can't become lucid in a dream, keep trying, but don't get too fixated on it. Give yourself time, and try out different techniques. Keep it light and fun. Sometimes the best things happen when we focus our intent but then relax and go with the flow. The great news is, the work we do with dreams when we're awake is like a waking version of lucid dreaming, and can be just as beneficial. All dreamwork is a sort of waking lucidity because we allow the dream to live, breathe, and develop by engaging consciously with its unconscious images and emotions, just as we can when we become lucid inside a dream. The more we practice waking lucidity by doing dreamwork and by following the "get lucid" techniques in this chapter, the more we are training ourselves to become lucidly aware in a dream.

### Lucid Dreamplay: the power of transformative dreamwork

As we've seen, in lucid dreams you can often guide and shape the dream just by intending to: calling out, "I'd like to see an elephant!" will very often result in the appearance of a dream elephant as lumbering and wrinkled as a real one. Dreams respond to our thoughts, emotions, and intentions, so if we want to resolve nightmares or heal from the past in a lucid dream, there are many ways of doing this.

But you don't have to be a lucid dreamer to benefit from your dreams in this way.

In fact, this book shows how you can experience the healing possibilities of lucid dreaming even if you haven't had a lucid dream yet.

The umbrella term for my key dreamwork tools and techniques is "Lucid Dreamplay." This is *lucid dreaming while awake*: working with a dream in ways that mirror the possibilities of lucid dreaming. We bring our attention to a dream and guide and shape it into something new. In Lucid Dreamplay, deep, unconscious dream imagery and the alert, awake mind interact to cocreate something new and valuable.

The beauty of Lucid Dreamplay is that anyone can do it. There are so many different options that you're bound to find at least a couple that work well for you. As you go through the book, you'll learn how to do the following types of Lucid Dreamplay, and more besides:

◊ Identify the healing energy, image, or symbol in dreams and nightmares
◊ Guide the dream towards transformation and healing
◊ Develop dream-inspired visualizations to reduce pain and ease physical illness
◊ Transform nightmares by moving the story forward

◊ Transcend a negative self-image
◊ Re-enter the dream to receive a teaching or a healing gift
◊ Absorb the highest energy or healing moment of the dream

One of my favorite Lucid Dreamplay techniques is Lucid Writing, which has helped many people to transform nightmares, identify the healing image in their dream, or create a vivid healing scenario.

## The transformative Lucid Writing technique

I created the Lucid Writing technique in 2003 as a creative tool while I was doing doctoral research into lucid dreaming. A waking version of lucid dreaming, it enables us to engage consciously with our deepest unconscious images and allow them to transform. Though I initially developed it as a creativity tool, as soon as I started teaching it in workshops I saw its healing potential: people would report recurring nightmares transforming into streams of healing imagery; psychological blocks dissolving as they wrote the dream into something new; and new insights and ideas emerging. For over a dozen years I've taught Lucid Writing in international workshops, and established psychotherapists have embraced it as a therapeutic dreamwork tool.

This simple technique builds on the concept of freewriting: writing without stopping in order to keep a connection with the unconscious. It tends to go much deeper than freewriting as it begins with a mind–body relaxation and visualization, and the core focus is always a dream, which means we have instant, direct contact with our unconscious images. When we work with our unconscious imagery and allow it to live and breathe and grow into something new, we are working on the most profound level of "reality creation", where we can guide our thoughts and internal imagery in healing ways to create our own best life.

Dream imagery can take you anywhere: into a childhood memory, a current life situation, or even into a fictional world as your imagination uses the dream imagery as a springboard into a story. With Lucid Writing, you can re-experience nightmares without fear and allow your unconscious to guide you into healing. All you need is paper, a pen, and a dream. It's important to write without stopping to think or critique what you are writing—just let it pour out of you, ungrammatical, badly spelled, and creative.

If you prefer not to write, you can choose any medium you like to follow on from this dreamplay: sketching, collaging, or speaking your impressions aloud into a recording device. Just make sure you have all the necessary materials right there before you sit down and start, otherwise you risk breaking the connection between you and your dream. Here are the steps into Lucid Writing. You can either memorize them to do alone, or ask a friend to read them to you as you go through the process.

## PRACTICE #18

### LUCID WRITING

1. **Choose a vivid dream** to work with.
2. **Identify the core image** at the heart of the dream. If it's a long, complicated dream with a confusing plot, choose one element or action where you feel strong emotion. Sometimes making up a short title for the dream can help you to identify its core.
3. **Sit comfortably** with a notebook and pen close at hand. Close your eyes.
4. **Breathe.** Feel your spine, straight but relaxed. Notice your breath moving in and out of your body. Take a few slow, deep breaths. Then inhale and turn your head to the right. Exhale as your head moves back to the center. Breathe in: turn your head to the left. Breathe out: return your head to the center. Continue

with this gentle breath-and-head movement for a short while, always breathing in at the center. Then relax.

5. **Visualize golden light.** With your eyes still closed, imagine a golden light gently flowing down over and through your body, warm and relaxing. It flows down over your head and shoulders, it flows down your spine, over your chest and into your belly. It flows over your hips and down through your legs, all the way to your feet. You are now encased in this golden light. Your eyes remain closed, and you can make a space in your mind: a safe, golden space.

6. **Bring your dream image into this space.** Focus on your dream image. Try to feel any emotions that come with it. Watch your dream image. Perhaps it will move and change into something else: you can let this happen. Just observe it calmly.

7. **Write without stopping.** When you feel ready, keep your dream imagery in your head and open your eyes ever so slightly. Take your pen and write *without stopping*. You might find yourself writing the dream imagery beyond itself, into something else: a new story, a new ending. Allow the imagery to develop in new directions if it wants to, and write down what happens. If you lose focus, simply return to the dream. Don't analyze what you write: let it flow and become whatever it wants to become. You might find yourself writing about a memory, or exploring your associations with one particular part of your dream. It's all good! As you write, breathe slowly and deeply, as if you're asleep. Write until it feels like you're done.

)———(

## Steve's nightmare: The Poisonous Snake

When Steve was on a tropical ecology field research expedition in Costa Rica, he had a nightmare about an extremely venomous viper, the fer-de-lance:

*I am in a cabin with some of my roommates, and a black fer-de-lance comes out of a corner of the room around my feet. I try to move away but it seems to follow me.*

The predominant emotion associated with Steve's nightmare was fear. He wanted to move beyond this primal fear reaction. In my workshop, I talked to the group about animals in dreams, and shared a lucid dream of my own where I found myself living in a jungle with a Bengal tiger. For the Lucid Writing exercise, I asked the workshop participants to mentally enter the skin of one of their dream animals and to speak with its voice. Steve became the poisonous snake:

*I am the fer-de-lance, hunting power embodied, focused and without fear. I am life itself, power and nourishment. But what is this strange place I have entered, and who is this being above me on this wooden floor? Certainly not dinner! Suddenly, I realize that I have a gift for this man, and I begin, laboriously, to work my way out from under this bed, and in a flash of golden light, we merge into one great and towering tree, fragrantly blossoming into a pure crystalline, golden orange and black Bengal tiger.*

## Steve's reflections on the Lucid Writing process

Lucid Writing as the dream animal was a powerful and healing experience for me. When I became the fer-de-lance, the real transformation took place. It was from the serpent's perspective that I realized the real reason I was moving towards the man (myself): I had a precious gift for him, if only he could overcome his fear and accept it.

I realized that the gift the fer-de-lance offered was animus energy, life itself, and an experience of our interconnectedness with the entire cosmos embodied in the tree of life. The Bengal tiger at the end felt like an integrative image which allowed me to affirm and honor the positive qualities of the fer-de-lance in myself, through the grace, boldness, and beauty of this giant cat Clare had offered to our group as one of her dream animals. The entire experience with these techniques served for me as a hero's journey of sorts, and I am most grateful for the wisdom and blessings Clare's written lucid dream re-entry techniques brought me.

---

Writing from a dream in this way goes beyond the majority of the techniques for understanding dreams that we looked at in chapter 2, because the aim of Lucid Writing is not only deeper understanding, but also inner transformation. When we actively re-enter a dream and then allow our conscious attention to engage with the flow of imagery, we enable powerful changes to take place in our inner movie. The effects can be startling and long lasting.

In Steve's imagination, he integrated with the snake and became first a tree of golden light, then a Bengal tiger. What had been a nightmare spontaneously transformed into healing imagery. Fear turned into joy. When we work with nightmares in this way, we can unwrap their gifts and claim them. Steve has created a fresh stream of healing imagery that he can draw on any time he needs to be reminded of his own grace, boldness, beauty, and connection with life.

You can easily do the same.

PRACTICE #19:

## INCUBATE A LUCID DREAM

1. Dream incubation is a time-honored practice that can be traced back several thousand years. This is a core technique that you'll find useful as you go through the book. When we want to dream of something in particular, it helps to bring a certain sense of ritual into it. You might want to write, "Tonight

I am lucid in my dreams" on a piece of paper and place it under your pillow, or have a long, candlelit bath before bed and meditate on becoming lucid in a dream. You could go to sleep holding a pebble in your fist and every time you feel it in the night, ask yourself if you are dreaming. Simply trying to hold onto the pebble through the night (and locating it each time you wake up) may help you to become lucid in a dream. The important thing is to set a firm intention to become lucid in your dreams tonight.

2. After turning out the light, lie in bed and vividly imagine becoming lucid in a dream. Where does your lucid dream take place? Who is present? What happens? You can use a nonlucid dream of your own and imagine what you would do if you became lucid in it. Tell yourself firmly, "Tonight, I will have a lucid dream."

3. As you drift off to sleep, try to remain aware by repeating, "I am dreaming. Everything I see is a dream. I am dreaming. . . ." so that you immediately enter a lucid dream. If this doesn't work at first, try steps 2 and 3 again after around five hours of sleep (set your alarm if you want to, or else just rely on the mini-awakenings we all have each night). Fully expect that you will wake up inside your dream!

)———(

# FOUR

# Transform your inner movie through Lucid Dreamplay

Dreams are inner movies that happen while we're asleep, but we have another movie reel spooling out all day long while we're wide awake. This is the movie we create as we go about our day. Our waking inner movie is made up of a rich mixture of thoughts, desires, fears, imaginings, reactions to people and events, worries, beliefs, assumptions, and expectations. The human brain is a magnificent thing. Alongside all its other tasks, it tackles the complex job of translating our interactions and external perceptions into some form of coherent inner experience. Perhaps it's no wonder that it tends to go into overdrive! Sometimes the constant stream of mental chatter going on in our heads each day is so familiar that we barely hear it any more.

This is where the danger begins because if we don't notice something, we can't change it. Often, unhelpful thoughts sneak into our minds and get absorbed into our inner movie in the form of negative mental images or limiting beliefs. Over time, they get stuck in our inner movie and take on cinematic power. Yet because they are largely unconscious, and because we don't pay close enough attention to the thoughts and images that move through our minds each day, we are generally unaware of their presence until things go wrong in our life. Without even realizing it, we have allowed something negative or otherwise limiting to become part of the way we view ourselves, our relationships with others, and our place in the world.

Our thoughts create our reality by shaping who we are. Who we are affects how we relate to others and the world. When our waking inner movie is constantly replaying negative images and limiting beliefs, we are unable to create our best life—the life we would love to have—because we are not yet our best self. But we can change things. When we modify our internal movies, we can become the creator of our own best life.

Mindful Dreaming can help us to change our inner movie. This chapter is about being psychologically aware and discovering that we have the power to change what we no longer need or want. Mindful Dreaming can help us to change the negativity that sometimes runs like a film in our brains: depressed thoughts, anxious thoughts, self-hating thoughts, judgements, doubts, and negative self-fulfilling prophesies. If you're thinking, "I really don't have any of that stuff running through my mind," that's wonderful to hear, but even the happiest people can slide into moments of self-doubt or negativity, so there's usually room for improvement. It's always worth paying attention to your personal inner movie of thoughts and imaginings as you go about your day. When you pay attention to what runs through your mind, you can instantly start the valuable work of modifying your inner movie for the better.

At the very least, you'll be practicing mindfulness, and the habit of thought-watching is great for triggering dream lucidity, too. Most importantly, you'll be giving yourself the chance to improve your life.

### Changing your inner movie can improve your life

Changing your inner movie helps you to:
1. Discard unhealthy mental patterns and improve the way you see yourself.

2. Remove self-fulfilling negative prophesies before they have a chance to germinate.

3. Allow new, happier possibilities to take place.

4. Get into a habit of positive thinking and creating pleasant mental scenarios.

5. Experience more moments of happiness in your day.

6. Move purposefully from anxious to calm, from resistant to flexible, from fragile to strong, from sad to happy.

7. Create your own best life. When you start to feel and think differently, you'll also change the vibe you give out, and people around you will respond to you more positively. You'll attract happier relationships and better situations. In doing so, you'll find yourself well on the way to creating the life you would love to live.

We *can* all guide our lives and create happiness; it's just that sometimes we don't know where to start. When we start with dreams, our own unconscious shows us what we need to do in order to change and heal.

Working with dreams is a wonderful way of returning to the self. Dreaming brings us into the heart of our own life. Dreams can help those who feel ready to change unhealthy relationship patterns, like a woman I worked with who finally plucked up the courage to shout at her abusive mother in a dream, "Hey, what the hell do you think you're doing?" Such dreams can be very powerful because they liberate abuse sufferers by proving to them not only that they can stand up for themselves, but that they are *worth* standing up for. When we take action in a dream, we are creating a blueprint for taking action in waking life. Our unconscious mind has experienced the possibility of change, and so it becomes easier to take the next step and translate this inner change into outer change. The cathartic experience of standing up to her mother in a dream laid the groundwork for this woman to become more assertive in her waking life.

Dreams can help people to climb out of psychological ruts and discard negative behavioural patterns. They can help people to throw off anxiety and fear so that they can become who they want to be. Many people today experience a lack of connection with the self. When we become disconnected from our own deep healing source, it's hard to be happy and healthy, because we don't understand what we really feel or need. But in actual fact, nobody can heal us better than we can heal ourselves: we are all healers because we are all dreamers, and dreams carry gifts of wisdom and healing. We just need to learn to listen to, and act upon, our dreams by doing Lucid Dreamplay.

The following practice is beneficial for anyone, but particularly for people who are suffering from anxiety or depression, as it builds up the skill of thought-watching so that we quickly learn to change negative or unhelpful thoughts into something brighter, enabling happiness to creep into our day.

PRACTICE #20

## EDIT YOUR WAKING INNER MOVIE: THE "CHANGE THAT THOUGHT!" TECHNIQUE

1. Practice mindfulness while awake by watching your thoughts. Start with just five minutes of thought-watching as you go about your usual activities.
2. As soon as you notice any negative thoughts, emotions, mental imagery, or scenarios creeping into your mind, identify them as unhelpful.
3. Then change these unhelpful components of your inner movie into something positive. An anxious inner scenario of fluffing what you want to say at an important meeting could be changed into a scenario where you express yourself with marvellous clarity. A feeling of anger due to someone else's behav-

iour can be diffused by trying to see their side of the situation, or simply recognizing that nobody is perfect and there's no point in dwelling on it.

4. Enjoy editing your inner movie; have fun with it and be creative! The whole point is to create a happier, more positive mental space from which to live your life.

5. Give yourself a smile and a mental pat on the back each time you're quick enough to modify negative thoughts in this way.

6. Do this exercise whenever you remember to during your day. Extend the time you do it from five minutes to ten, then longer. Over time, it will become automatic to correct unhelpful thoughts, attitudes, and imaginings. Your daytime inner movie will improve, and you'll become more mindful, more focused, and more positive.

7. By changing your daytime movie, you'll change your dreams, too. You'll find yourself questioning unpleasant dream scenes and emotions, and this can trigger more lucid dreams, as well as spontaneously causing the dream story to change for the better.

)———(

## How to become more self-aware

Each of us carries different selves within us. We were a certain way when we were five and completely different again when we were fifteen, or twenty-five. Sometimes we have forgotten or disowned some of our selves. Yet these younger selves still live on inside us and can affect our current behaviour and reactions, so that for example we might experience violent emotions that are completely out of proportion to a situation, simply because of events that have upset us in the past, perhaps without us ever being fully aware of them. Becoming more psychologically self-aware is the first step to psychological healing.

Dreams are mirrors; they skip from past to present to future, showing us where we came from, who we are today, and where we're going. This next exercise is a playful way of recognizing the different selves we carry within us and accepting them as part of who we are, but crucially also learning to spot them the moment they raise their heads so that we can move towards new, happier ways of being in the world.

## PRACTICE #21

### THE FIVE "ME'S"

1. Pick five different ages in your life that correspond to different levels of your development. For example, the first might be you as a young child, the second as a teenager, the third in your twenties, and the last two at different major stages in your life, such as the age you were when you suffered a serious illness or loss, fell in love for the first time, or traveled around the world.

2. Take a sheet of paper and write your five ages down, leaving a generous space under each one. For each different age write a quick list of words or short phrases that describe yourself at that age in terms of emotions, behaviour, fears, obsessions, hurts, and desires. Include any major memories from that age if you feel they shaped your outlook on life.

3. When you're done, give each "me" a name that perfectly encapsulates its energy. Be playful; let your imagination loose. When I do this exercise with creative writing groups, it's fascinating to hear how people name their various inner selves: Hippy-Chick; Daredevil; Pressure-Cooker; The Lonely One; Diva; Mr. Organized; The "Gimme Love" Boy.

4. You should now have five "me's." Congratulations! Look at how complex you are and see how much you've changed already in your life. Take a moment to appreciate your qualities and

notice your less lovely tendencies, without judgement. Accept yourself compassionately for who you are, while remembering that you can change anything about yourself that you would like to change.

5. Now write one more paragraph, this time about your ideal "me." Who is the "me" that you would really love to be? Let this best version of yourself come to life on the page. Is she braver, more tactful, than your current self? Does he have greater social ease, nicer friends? Allow yourself to dream your best self into being. Have fun with it.

)———(

Seeing how much we've changed already in our life reminds us that *we can always change.* Why not decide that the next change will be a beautiful, positive one? Becoming more self-aware can help us to embrace the parts of ourselves that we want to flourish and diffuse our habitual negative responses such as lashing out in anger or feeling victimized. When we notice, "Uh-oh, my inner diva has just woken up!" we can take steps to calm down instead of screeching at someone we love.

Little by little, we step forward into our best self.

### Improving a negative body image

Unhealthy mental patterns and self-perceptions can be changed. So much depends on becoming aware of our inner movie of thoughts, judgements, and self-criticisms, and then changing them for the better. A young woman came to a one-off yoga and dream-writing day I was running. I asked her my usual question, "Have you done any yoga before?" In response, she gestured towards her body. "No," she said, "I never do any exercise—can't you tell?" She began to cry, apologizing for her tears and saying how depressed she felt, being so overweight. She wasn't even that heavy! I said to this lovely, fragile woman, "We are so much more than our bodies. The body is just a shell we wear throughout life. Yes, we need to take care of it, as poor health is no fun, but it's a big mistake to identify ourselves as being only 'this body.' What we *really* are is spirit and soul."

I invited her to do yoga. Yoga is a wonderful way of connecting mind, body, and spirit, and of feeling a greater acceptance of one's body. Afterwards, everyone did Lucid Dreamplay where they transformed and transcended their body image, as in the exercise below. At the end of the day the young woman told me she was determined to begin a regular yoga practice and start keeping a dream diary.

### PRACTICE #22

## TRANSCENDING OUR BODY IMAGE

1. Close your eyes. Can you remember a dream where you were aware of your body? If so, summon a mental image of your body as it looked and felt in your dream. If you can't think of a dream, just picture your body as it looks today. You can imagine yourself naked or with clothes on.

2. Focus on the image of your body: how exactly does it look and feel? Notice any emotions that come up, without allowing them to break your focus.

3. Now summon a feeling of love in your heart and picture light surrounding this image of your body.

4. Allow the image to transform if it wants to. The idea here is not to visualize the body of a tanned model in a swimsuit and mentally stick our own head on top of it. It's to transcend any negativity we may hold about our body, and perhaps transcend the body image itself by moving through it into other imagery, without prior expectations.

5. Watch the image transform in spontaneous ways. One woman saw herself turn into a lynx with a lustrous pelt and hypnotic green eyes. Her visualization connected her with her powerful animal nature and reminded her that her green eyes were her best feature. A man saw himself with a beating, golden heart. This reminded him of his own compassionate nature. There may be no transformation of imagery; you might simply experience a sensation of love or acceptance towards your body. The harder this exercise is for you, the more beneficial it will be for you to repeat it until you feel a powerful resonance with any positive sensation or imagery.

6. Return when you are ready, by opening your eyes. Thank your body for all that it does for you. Appreciate that it carries you through life, while recognizing that you are more than your body—you are spirit and soul.

7. Afterwards, every time you notice yourself thinking a negative thought about your body, recall your positive, healing self-image and say your name mentally to anchor it to your sense of self. Changing our waking inner movie by working with positive self-imagery can have a transformative effect on our lives and relationships.

)———(

Dreams can help us to change our old self-image for a more positive one. Allow your dreams to bring you into contact with your eternal self; the you that shines out from your eyes and from the energy that you bring into the world. Labeling ourselves in negative ways so that we think of ourselves as "the overweight woman" or "the ugly man" is not only a deeply unhelpful inner movie to play; on a spiritual level, it is also fundamentally untrue. Imagine relabeling yourself as "the woman with beautiful green eyes" or "the man with a heart of gold." Doesn't that instantly feel better? The more we believe in our own labeling, the faster our inner movie will transform. We'll find our self-perception, our behaviour, and the way others relate to us changing, too. We will become our best selves.

Having a negative self-image is just one aspect of ourselves that we can change by working on our inner movie. Today, many people suffer from depression, phobias, and anxiety. Dreamworkers, psychologists, and psychotherapists have found that healing dream imagery can help people out of depressed states.

### How Mindful Dreaming can help with depression, anxiety, and phobias

Dreams can be very intense. They can arrive in a flood that is hard to take. Fiona, who was suffering from depression and anxiety, reflects on how intense and disturbing her dreamlife became during that period. She points out that each wave of upsetting dreams arrived just before a shift to a more positive stage in her process of battling the depression:

> I dreamed that I was strangling and suffocating myself, woke up screaming and not knowing where I was. In another dream, I dreamed I was drowning. In between the shifts things got very intense. I felt incompetent (like I was dying) and like I was hurting myself. These were just brief phases while I moved through the next lot of stuff and shifted to a new place, but they felt very difficult, intense, and emotionally draining. Often I just wanted it all to stop.

For fifty years, we've known that clinically depressed people spend more time in REM sleep and dream much more than other people do. One important function of dreaming is to free us from toxic emotions, so isn't it a good thing that depressed people dream more? Unfortunately it might not be, because, in doing so, they may miss out on vital deep sleep.

In a 2003 interview in the *New Scientist*, psychologist Joe Griffin discusses how he and his colleagues found that in people with clinical depression, the emotional safety net that dreams provide has gone into overdrive. Because a major symptom and cause of depression is worrying about problems to the extent of feeling hopelessness, the dreaming mind tries extra hard to process all these strong emotions at night. Unfortunately, this can mean that the depressed person is spending much more time than they should be in the highly active state of REM sleep. A healthy young adult normally spends around 25 percent of the night in REM sleep, and 75 percent in deep, recuperative sleep.

A depressed person, however, may dream up to three times more than this! At these levels, he or she is over-dreaming and so is missing out on vital, restorative sleep.

The result? The depressed person wakes up exhausted.

When we wake up exhausted, the last thing we feel able to do is bounce out of bed and seek creative answers to our problems. Instead, we worry about them even more, and the unresolved worry—over-dreaming—daytime exhaustion cycle continues. We remain depressed. This was Fiona's problem—she was over-dreaming and it was leaving her exhausted. The combination of an onslaught of unpleasant dreams and not enough deep sleep wore her down and sometimes she felt as though she was going mad.

Joe Griffin stresses that the most important thing clinically depressed people can do if they find they are over-dreaming is anything that stops them from worrying and ruminating on their problems. Seeing a therapist who can help them to find practical and emotional tools with which to face their life problems can be very helpful, but sometimes simply understanding *why* they are over-dreaming is enough for many people to free themselves from this cycle.

When people are able to stop worrying so much about their problems, their dreaming sleep rapidly returns to its normal, helpful levels. They wake up feeling refreshed and recover the mental strength they need to face their lives and resolve their problems. People with depression should try to get deep relaxation as often as they can. Simply lying quietly and listening to a guided deep relaxation visualization every day can help the body to get the recuperative rest it so desperately needs.

Fiona found that a combination of writing down and talking about her dreams, having sessions with a life coach, and listening to relaxation CDs helped her to get through this intense period of dreaming and throw off her anxiety and depression. Her sleep is no longer disturbed by nightmares.

Dreams act as a barometer of our emotional life. If something is wrong, a dream appears to let us know that we need to act to change things.

## Working with healing dream imagery to alleviate depression

The cofounder of the Dream Research Institute in London, psychotherapist Dr. Nigel Hamilton, worked with a depressed schizoid man who hadn't been held or touched by his mother for two years. The man dreamed that a very wise crimson parrot in a cage was looking at him intently. He felt a profound sense of connection with the bird. Soon afterwards, the man dreamed of two caged animals with magical qualities. Using visualizations, he worked on incorporating these wise dream animals into his sense of self. Finally, the man dreamed of a luminous white orb descending into a lattice cage. He opened the cage and bit into the orb. It tasted like a revitalizing elixir.

Through working with his powerful healing dream imagery, the man had reconnected with a part of himself that had been locked away. In his 2016 International Association for the Study of Dreams (IASD) presentation on "Luminescent Colors in Lucid Dreams and Visions," Dr. Hamilton reported that following this dreamwork, the man has now overcome his depressed schizoid state and has reconnected with the family he was alienated from.

Changing the dream through lucid dreaming is ideal therapy for depression. In *The Effect of Intentional Dreaming on Depression*, Jungian analyst Francis Manley found that when people suffering from depression were taught to consciously influence their dreams for positive outcomes, such as confronting a nightmarish figure and changing it into something healing, they began to gain more control over their waking lives, too. It is pivotal for those suffering from depression to take an active role in their waking life. Lucid dreaming and its waking counterpart, Lucid Dreamplay, can help us to practice forms of positive action to propel us towards psychological change. When we change our dreams, we change our lives: this is the power of lucid dreaming and Lucid Dreamplay.

When we work to absorb our own personal healing dream imagery, we are nourishing ourselves on a profound level. This can have transformative effects on our relationships with others and on our own mental state.

## A way out of depression: how dreams illuminate solutions

Dreams often illuminate obstacles: they show us emotional blocks, or feelings of powerlessness or hopelessness. But just as often, dreams illuminate solutions, and when we do healing work with the dream, we understand what needs to be done to improve our situation. Let's look at Bonnie's dream to see this process in action. Bonnie was depressed because of a distressing ongoing situation with her daughter-in-law. Then she had this archetypal dream, which illuminated a solution by showing her there is more than one way to react to the problem.

## Bonnie's dream: Rescue through
## Spiritual and Practical Means

*I am with a group of women in simple garb, like in biblical times. It's a barren place with cliffs. There are women and children but no men. I am terribly exhausted and wonder if I can make it physically, but I am surviving.*

*Then a five-year-old girl falls off the cliff and into the river.*

*The priestess stops and goes into the prayer position. Another woman pulls out a woven basket like an organic net, attached to a long stick. She goes into the river and gets the little girl out.*

At the time of this dream, in my waking life I was depressed and feeling bad that my daughter-in-law had told my son that she was still angry with me for not making her feel welcome when she first came to the US.

Your workshop really was the healing because I experienced it in my body. I went back into the dream, and I was first the little girl who was rescued. I experienced being scooped up out of the water and being held (hugged). I then became the little girl's mother. I went to the child and held her. Then the priestess and the rescuer formed a circle around us and came close. And then the whole tribe stood around us in a close circle. The emotion rose up through my body and the tears flowed. This release of emotions and feeling it in my body was the healing.

In my workshop, I asked Bonnie what she had been doing to improve the difficult situation with her daughter-in-law. She said that she had been praying and visualizing that the situation would improve. Struck by the similarity between Bonnie's prayers and the way the priestess in her dream went into the prayer position, I asked her what she thought might have happened in the dream if all of the women had fallen to their knees and prayed like the priestess, and nobody had taken practical steps to save the child. Would the little girl have been OK, or would she have been swept away by the river? Perhaps prayer alone is not always enough? Sometimes we need to take practical action in order to reach out to somebody.

Bonnie's dream illuminates how well the spiritual and practical members of the group of women work together. If Bonnie's dream women are viewed as different aspects of her—the spiritual and practical aspects—it appears that she already possesses the tool she needs to reach out to her daughter-in-law; she just needs to work out what it is. Afterwards, that's exactly what Bonnie did. She reports, "I had some insights after the healing in your workshop. I think that being able to spend time together to get to know each other would really be the best solution. I remind myself to just reach out and that is what really counts. I can't control her response. As you said, I have the tool."

In line with the message of her dream, Bonnie has found a highly *practical* way of reaching out to her daughter-in-law: she plans to spend more time with her and get to know her better. With a little goodwill and understanding, both women may be able to make the other feel seen and cared about. Inner change equals outer change. When we do healing dreamwork, we release our power to change our lives.

The following dreamwork practice can feel very healing, and it's great if you need support and a listening ear.

## PRACTICE #23

### SHARE A DREAM WITH A FRIEND

Simply being heard is incredibly therapeutic. If you are working with an extremely frightening or upsetting dream, it is advisable to find an experienced therapist to talk to about it. Otherwise, try this exercise with a trusted friend. It works best with fairly short dreams, not epic ones that take ten minutes to relate!

1. Tell your dream to your friend. There is no need for anyone to try and interpret the dream. The friend only listens.
2. Now listen to your friend sharing their own dream. Listen attentively, without saying a word.
3. Tell each other *the same dream* again. (Now you see why it's best to stick to short dreams for this exercise.) Often, when we tell the dream a second time, something changes; we remember something we'd forgotten, or get a new insight, or become aware of a particular emotion. Again, only listen; don't comment yet.
4. When you have both shared your dream twice, talk with your friend and see if your feelings about your respective dreams have shifted in any way. Now is the time when clarifying questions, insights, or reactions to each other's dream can be exchanged if it feels right. Remember, the dream belongs to the dreamer, so be respectful and don't be tempted to force your interpretation of your friend's dream onto them. The most important thing is to care for each other's dreams by listening to them in a warm, supportive way. It can feel very healing to share dreams.

)———(

## Lucid Dream Therapy for anxiety and phobias

A review of thirteen separate studies in the *Journal of Anxiety Disorders* by researchers Mark Powers and Paul Emmelkamp from the University of Amsterdam showed that Virtual Reality Exposure Therapy (VRET) is highly effective in treating anxiety disorders and phobias. The sufferer is given a virtual reality headset and gradually gets used to feeling calm while experiencing simulations of stress-triggering situations such as standing on a high bridge if they have a fear of heights.

In terms of realism, lucid dreaming goes far beyond the reach of virtual reality. When we become lucid in a dream, we are 100 percent immersed in a fabulously real inner world. Lucid dreaming could help people to overcome phobias by using a technique similar to VRET, where the lucid dreamer asks to meet the thing she or he is frightened of: snakes, bats, heights. People with severe phobias that affect their ability to live a normal life should always see a therapist before attempting self-therapy, but lucid dreaming has helped even fairly strong phobias to disappear. In an article, "How to Cure Fears and Phobias with Lucid Dreaming," Rebecca Turner describes the experience of Madeleine Hopkins, who was phobic about spiders. Madeleine successfully desensitized herself by handling a spider in a lucid dream:

> It takes courage, but I know when I wake up I'll be annoyed if I wimped out, so I poke my finger into the web and touch a spider. It crawls onto my finger. I hold my finger up. The spider is wrapped up in its own web but it wriggles free and walks along my finger. I feel no fear or horror. I feel proud of myself.

The next day, Madeleine was able—while awake—to let a spider crawl right up her arm! This would have been unthinkable for her before the lucid dream. Other people have overcome their fear of plane travel, the dark, and heights in lucid dreams. Lucid dreaming mirrors a virtual reality platform where exposure therapy can be used to face fears, anxieties, and phobias.

## How to find the healing element in dreams

Some dreams may have a clear healing element, such as light, nature, beautiful imagery, feelings of happiness or joy, or pleasurable sensations such as flying or sexual ecstasy. In her article

"The Healing Power of Dreams and Nightmares," Wendy Pannier, past president of the IASD, shares a dream she had after having surgery for cancer:

> It is night and everything is black. All of a sudden ahead of me I see a tree that is totally lit up. It is full of different kinds of birds and animals in the most vibrant iridescent colors—the most vivid shades I have ever seen. I am in awe of the incredible life and vitality of the creatures in the tree. It is like a "tree of life" and it feels very positive.

It's easy to spot the healing elements in Wendy's dream: vibrant colors, vital creatures. Everything in this dream sings with life. But many dreams may be less positive, and the healing nature of the dream may be less obvious at first. A fifty-year-old friend of mine who was emerging from a divorce dreamed she was wearing a terribly tight bone corset that was very uncomfortable and was preventing her from breathing freely. In the dream, she saw a changing room and moved towards it so that she could remove the corset. Can you find a healing element in this dream?

It could be the changing room as this is somewhere we can feel free to *change*; restrictive behaviours and beliefs can be stripped off. But the corset might also be considered the healing image, as although it is uncomfortably tight, it is an active force pushing the dreamer towards transformation. Sometimes forces in our lives push us towards wholeness and healing by making us seek change (a changing room). Only the dreamer of this dream can really know which element in her dream is the healing one. It's good to remember that *in every dream of your own, you will instinctively know which the healing element is, as it will resonate with you.* When my friend and I talked about her dream, it made us think of an unhatched butterfly getting ready to break out of its restrictive chrysalis and fly away on brand new wings.

Not all healing dreams may seem positive at first. Often they come in the form of nightmares. Nightmares can be pretty loud. They want our attention, and they want it now. The nightmare shouts, "Healing is needed!" A woman in my workshop dreamed she was wrestling with an alligator, turning over and over in the water, struggling and half-drowning. In the dream, she knew she had to kill the alligator in order to extract a healing elixir from inside his belly. This dream came when she was battling illness, and she felt the dream was showing her that she had to find healing "inside." Every dream has some healing potential, and nightmares can be a particularly rich source of healing once we know the best techniques with which to work with them. There's a golden rule about dreams to keep in mind: all dreams have healing potential. When we do dreamwork, we begin the process of turning the dream into a healing dream.

In cases where the healing element of the dream isn't immediately obvious, we can tease it out by working with it in different ways while awake. Emotions can be powerful tools for healing, so watch out for these as they appear in your dreams. For example, if someone has trouble expressing anger and spends a lifetime swallowing down angry remarks and avoiding confrontation, a healing dream for them might be one in which they bellow in rage! It's good not to be too quick to dismiss a dream as negative or as not containing a healing element.

When we learn how to identify the healing image in a dream, we can work on integrating this positive imagery into our lives so that it transforms us for the better. Here's an easy technique to identify the healing image or emotion in your dream.

## PRACTICE #24

## FIND THE HEALING IMAGE

Sit calmly. Re-enter your dream imaginatively, with your eyes closed. Allow the dream to build around you so you can see it clearly. You feel completely safe to explore the imagery, knowing you can stop this process at any time by opening your eyes. As you watch your dream unfold, stay alert for the central image, symbol, or emotion. You are looking for the healing element of this dream—it might be some light, something in nature, or maybe it's something negative that you sense has the power to propel you into healing. The healing image or energy may not be what you expect, so just allow the dream imagery to transform if it wants to, to show you a healing possibility.

When you feel ready, describe your healing image to yourself in one sentence, perhaps giving it a title. Then take a deep breath and open your eyes, returning to the room with your healing dream image. Sketch it or write it down so that it stays with you. Well done if you managed to find a healing image with your first attempt at this exercise. If you didn't, don't worry; just try it again with a different dream.

In one workshop I led where we did this exercise, many people found their dark or menacing dream images spontaneously transformed into new, happier scenes. The titles they gave their healing images revealed the transformation. A dream of a demon became "A Demon Turns into Healing Gold." A dream of a dark tower became "Light Enters the Tower." Notice the way that solutions are found; fearsome beings or dark spaces transform into positive imagery and light. This transformation should never be forced, or it will have little power. Usually the simple act of working with a dream in the hope of healing will enable a spontaneous transformation of the imagery to take place. In dreams, we come face to face with our deepest unconscious images. When we shine a light onto dreams by thinking about them and working with them, we illuminate these unconscious images and enable them to transform.

This final short practice shows how to integrate the most beautiful, healing imagery from our dreams and our Lucid Dreamplay into our lives. Use this practice as many times a day as you want. Introduce other happy images or feelings to it whenever you can. Life is made of moments, so every happy moment you can add to your day is worth it.

The more happy moments you create in your day, the happier your life will become.

### PRACTICE #25

## TAKE A HEALING BREATH

This quick practice can be done anytime, anywhere. It can be done while grabbing a latte, or buttoning your coat. It can be done while you're in the elevator, or frying an egg. It takes under thirty seconds. Yet the beauty of this exercise is that the more often you do it, the more your life will change for the better. This is a mood-lifter that can bring solace, courage, and joy into the moments of your daily life.

1. Choose a healing dream image for the week (or for the whole month). This can come directly from a dream, or from any transformative Lucid Dreamplay you have done with the dream.
2. Vividly recall your healing dream image and take a deep breath. Imagine that you are breathing your image right into

your body just as we breathe in oxygen through our lungs, which is then taken to every cell in the body. Feel the strength and energy of your healing image filling you.

3. As you breathe out, release any sadness or upset.

4. Breathe in again and imagine your healing image illuminating your body like warm light.

5. Smile and breathe out.

6. That's all!

)———(

# FIVE

# Sexual dreams for health and well-being

We all have sexual energy. Without a sex drive, the human race would have died out long ago, along with most of the animal kingdom. Sexual desire is hardwired into every one of us and must be expressed; yet it's the most repressed, maligned, and taboo form of human energy that exists. Sexual energy is a vital life force, and it is not always expressed through the sexual act. Sometimes it's expressed through creativity, other times through desire in its many forms: the desire to possess, the desire to protect, the desire to be gratified. Sexual energy can also lead to soul-enhancing experiences of extraordinary depth, especially when combined with dreams.

We are all sexually aroused when we dream. Most dreams tend to occur in REM sleep. In his 2011 article "The Very, Very Strange Properties of REM Sleep." Dr. Patrick McNamara explains that REM sleep first paralyzes, then sexually activates the sleeper before dreaming begins. Plenty of odd things happen inside our bodies while we are in REM sleep: we all enter physical paralysis, to stop us from leaping out of bed and acting out our dreams, but at the same time, our heart rate accelerates, our brain temperature rises, we experience muscle twitches, abnormal breathing patterns, and automatic nervous system "storms." On top of all that, the penis or clitoris becomes aroused. And then what happens? We begin to dream. Against such a crazy physiological backdrop, it hardly seems surprising that dreams can be so bizarre, so realistic, and so sexy.

We can experience physical orgasms while dreaming an erotic dream. Dream orgasms, both male and female, have been recorded in sleep laboratories. While men's wet dreams give external proof that dream orgasms can be as real in a physical sense as waking ones, when female lucid dreamers are attached to vaginal probes while having dream sex, they too show physical signs of actual orgasm. Research conducted by psychophysiologists Stephen LaBerge and Walter Greenleaf in 1983 recorded the first lucid dream orgasm. Having found a lover in her lucid dream, the subject, Beverly D'Urso, used specific, pre-agreed eye movements to signal the onset of orgasm. Simultaneously, her vaginal blood flow, vaginal muscle activity, and respiration rate all reached their highest levels of that night. Sexual dreams are highly realistic. Whether we are sexually repressed, shy, or wish we were having more sex, dreams give us a safe environment to experiment and enjoy our own sexual energy. We can't get STDs from dream sex!

Sometimes there will be no need to work with a sexual dream in order to understand what it is telling us, even if we have unconsciously hidden that knowledge from ourselves. Sexual dreams can be complex, as they can cover such a wide range of emotions and situations. They can make us wake up shuddering with pleasure or disgust. They can bring to light happy memories or traumas. They can reveal to us the state of our relationships with others, and with our own body. Sexual dreams can be unwrapped through Lucid Dreamplay techniques like the ones given throughout this book, and if we want more sexual dreams, all we have to do is ask for them by incubating a dream.

As we go through life, sexual awakenings can reflect a larger awakening; a change coming in our life. So if we are happily married and suddenly find ourselves fantasizing or dreaming about another person, it doesn't necessarily mean that we are bored with our spouse and want to be with this other person. Our desire might reflect inner changes such as a longing for new possibilities (a career change, another baby, a more spiritual life, greater health and vitality, new friends).

But how can we know if our sexual energy is trying to tell us to switch jobs, heal past rifts, or start taking meditation classes?

Easy: we look to our dreams for guidance.

## A guide to understanding sex dreams

◊ **A sex dream may not be about sex.** If you dream of having sex with a stranger, this may symbolize that a new aspect of yourself is emerging or that you are open to something new and unknown. The inability to complete sex in a dream, whether due to interruptions or impotence, could reflect a waking life situation where you feel unable to complete something. Many people dream of having sex with people who they actually know, and often they find this bewildering, embarrassing, or shameful. But from a psychological point of view, dreaming of having sex with someone you know does not necessarily mean you want to have sex with them in waking life. It might mean that you feel attracted to a certain quality they have. Try asking yourself, "What do I admire about this person?"

If this is hard to work out because you dreamed you were having sex with a colleague who you dislike, for example, describe them in short phrases and then see if any of their qualities or abilities appeal to you. Be specific, and try to be fair—everyone has some good qualities (talks too loudly; arrogant; knows what he wants; socially at ease; rock-climber . . .). Your description might lead to the recognition that although this person irritates you, you wish you had their social ease or adventurous spirit.

Sexual energy is a very alive, active energy. Once you have identified the wished-for quality that this energy is focusing on, you can begin to actively incorporate it into your self-perception and develop it, for example by signing up for an activity that you consider adventurous. By acting on this particular quality, you take the first step towards owning it.

◊ **Emotions are key in sexual dreams.** After a sex dream, ask yourself, "How did I feel during the dream?" If your feelings changed during the dream, did they change for the better or worse? If dream sex is mind-numbingly boring and mechanical, this may reflect an inner need to change something in order to make your life exciting and stimulating again.

A common sex dream is of being caught in the act; during exuberant, orgasmic sex, the bedroom door opens and there stands a deeply disapproving person—your mother or your old school teacher. In dreams where the emotions crash from bliss to shock or shame, it's worth seeing if there is a bridge to events in your waking life. Ask yourself, "Where in my life have I experienced similar emotions?" If the person at the door reminds you of anyone, think about your response to this person—are you letting someone (or something) in your life spoil your fun?

◊ **Witnessing sexual dreams.** In some sexual dreams, we are not involved in the action: we are watching it. Again, notice how you feel in the dream. Are you involved? Do you feel left out? Do you feel curious about what these dream lovers are doing together? Are you turned on? Make the bridge to your waking life. Are you currently getting enough sex? Are you holding back from sex? Are you keen to experiment more in bed? Sometimes dreams offer us a safe space to learn more about sexual possibilities. They allow us to release our inhibitions and discover our inner desires. If you watch erotic movies, this type of witnessing dream may simply be your dreaming mind reenacting waking life experiences.

◊ **Rape in dreams.** When sex or sexual contact in dreams is nonconsensual, this can have many different levels of possible meaning. The way to find out its significance is to do dreamwork, but if you are plagued by repetitive rape nightmares, please see a qualified therapist: it may indicate past sexual trauma and you will need care and support when unwrapping these dreams. Rape dreams may be symbolic, indicating that we feel violated in some area of our life, or they may reflect our conflicting feelings about an emotionally or physically abusive relationship or with the opposite sex in general.

At its highest, sex is ecstatic union. At its lowest, it is violent coercion. The appearance of rape in a dream (whether the dreamer is being raped, witnessing rape, or is the rapist) may be a red flag that there is an unconscious rift or imbalance that needs to be healed. The following practices can help: "Forgive—Love—Release" (page 117); "How to transform nightmares" (page 125); the "Love and Light transformative technique" (page 147); and "Colored breathing for emotional safety" (page 101).

◊ **Releasing pent-up sexual desire.** Dreams offer us a safe outlet for brimming-over sexual desire. Sexual dreams might be compensating for a dry period in our sex life, or they might indicate a general desire for intimacy or emotional love. Studies have shown that women have more sex dreams around the time of ovulation, which makes perfect biological sense, as this is the best time to get pregnant. Sex dreams may therefore have no particular meaning. They may simply be an overflow of sexual energy.

◊ **Sexual orientation dreams.** Dreams can help us to understand and embrace our own sexual orientation. In dreams,

we can experiment with same-sex partners as well as
experiencing ourselves as male, female, or hermaphrodite.
Lucid dreams have special potential for those exploring
their sexual orientation because when we wake up in a
dream we can ask to experience any kind of sex or intimate situation we are interested in, knowing that we are
safe and in a private world. When we wake up, these
dreams can be worked with using techniques such as
Lucid Writing, for greater self-understanding, wholeness,
and self-acceptance.

Sexual boundaries in dreams are fluid. If we think of
ourselves as heterosexual and dream about having homo-
sexual sex, this does not necessarily mean we are having
doubts about our sexual orientation (although it might); it
could point to the need for a deeper and more balanced
union of the feminine and masculine energies (or what
Jung would refer to as the anima and animus archetypes)
we all have within us. Doing Lucid Dreamplay is the way
to find out.

◊ **Dreams signposting health and disease in the sexual
organs.** After a hysterectomy, one woman worried that
from now on, she would be devoid of all sexual pleasure.
Then she dreamed that she had a wonderful orgasm. The
dream showed her very literally that her sex drive and
ability to feel sexual pleasure remained healthy. Other
dreams may flag disease in the sexual organs: another lady
in one of my workshops told me she dreamed she was
peeing fire. It turned out she had cystitis. Chapter 8 has
more examples of dreams warning of disease in the body.

◊ **Dreams of a partner's infidelity.** Sexual dreams can reveal
things we were not consciously aware of, but not all
dreams of infidelity point to an actual infidelity, so be care-
ful about leaping to conclusions. A dream that your lover
is cheating on you could reflect that you are currently feel-

ing unloved or unsupported by them, or it could be high-lighting another area of your life where you feel betrayed or disrespected. Focus on the emotions within your dream, and do Lucid Dreamplay to discover more.

◊ **Dreaming of an ex-lover.** People often dream of sleeping with ex-lovers. This could mean that they are processing and accepting what they have learned from them and releasing old ties to move on with their lives. Then again, the dream may be trying to tell you that you still have feelings for your ex. Examine your emotions in the dream. Is it a tender encounter? Awkward? Purely sexual? If you are not sure what your dream means, do try the "Dream Talk technique" (page 38) to find out more and ask for a clarifying dream by writing in your dream journal, "I'd like a dream to help me understand the meaning of this dream."

◊ **Dreams of a current sexual partner.** When we dream of our current sexual partner, we can discover how we really feel about a relationship. Over a decade ago, I was at an IASD dream conference in the US. At breakfast I was sitting with a lovely group of dreamworkers, psychoanalysts, and authors. When they learned that I had gotten married ten weeks earlier, someone asked me if I often dreamed of my husband. As it happened, I'd dreamed of him that night, and I told them the dream: *It's a sunny day and we are walking into the sparkling sea together, holding hands. As we get deeper into it, the waves get bigger. It's exciting and a little scary. We tumble through the waves, still holding hands.*

The psychotherapist next to me asked, "How were you tumbling?"

Without thinking, I replied, "Oh, just sort of . . . head over heels."

Everyone within earshot laughed and as I grasped what I'd said, I groaned—how corny! I apologized for putting them off their breakfast with my head-over-heels-in-love newlywed dream. Just asking one well-aimed question about the dream can trigger deeper understanding.

◊ **Lucid sex dreams.** When you become lucid in a dream, you can guide and shape the dream if you want to. Many lucid dreamers experiment with sexual encounters in their dreams. The advantage of a lucid dream is that you can recall your desire for dream sex as soon as you recognize that you are dreaming, and then put it into action by a) calming your emotions so that the dream scene remains stable and you don't wake up; b) announcing your intention to have dream sex; and c) fully expecting the perfect dream lover to come along.

Expectation is important in lucid dreams: when you fully expect your own idea of a sex god or goddess to appear in the dream and want to have sex with you, it is much more likely to happen than if you half-heartedly hope that someone sexy might happen along in the dream. Spending time visualizing your ideal dream sex scenario before going to sleep can help it to become a reality in both nonlucid and lucid dreams.

◊ **Spiritual sexual dreams.** Sexual energy in dreams can lead to profound spiritual experiences. In many of her sexual lucid dreams, clinical psychologist Patricia Garfield finds herself dissolving into brilliant beauty and light at the moment of orgasm. In one lucid dream, she was twirling around on a trapeze bar when suddenly she plunged downwards, burst into orgasm, and experienced a rapturous pattern of colors. Such dreams helped her to understand that sexual arousal can show us the strength of our own life force and even lead to mystical experiences. When we learn to ride the wave of sexual desire in dreams, it can take us to deeply satisfying, orgasmic experiences that leave us refreshed and energized upon waking. This is something to try in a lucid dream if the idea appeals to you.

## PRACTICE #26

### INCUBATE A SEXUAL DREAM

Thinking about sex gives you sex dreams. A 2009 study of seventy students by German psychologist Michael Schredl and colleagues asked about their waking life sexual behaviour and their dream content. The results clearly showed that the number of erotic dreams we have is not related to how often we have sex or how often we masturbate. It is related to how much time we spend engaged in sexual fantasies during the day. So if you want more dream sex, spend more time fantasizing about sex!

1. Try sleeping naked or in sexy underwear so that, whenever you wake briefly during the night, you are reminded of your goal to have a sexual dream.
2. After turning out the light, lie in bed and indulge in a fantasy about the kind of erotic dream you would like to have tonight. Imagine it vividly, in as much color and detail as you can. Where does it take place? Who is present? What happens? Play out your fantasy from start to finish, and then tell yourself, "Tonight, I will have this dream."
3. As you drift off to sleep, try to remain aware by repeating, "I am dreaming. Everything I see is a dream. I am dreaming . . ." Do this every time you wake up during the night. If you become lucid in a dream, you can remember your goal and pursue your fantasy. Even if you don't have a lucid dream, if you have followed these dream incubation steps, you are likely to have a sexual dream during the night.

)———(

## *Too much dream sex?*

As we've seen, physical arousal is normal for everyone while we are dreaming, and this can lead to highly sexualized dreams. You may think, "Where's the problem? Dream sex is great!" But too much sexual energy can feel overwhelming. Recently, a young woman approached me saying that she was scared to have lucid dreams as she would experience such strong sexual energy. Let's have a look at her experiences.

---

### Katie's sexual lucid dreams

My lucid dreams involve a tremendous amount of what feels like sexual energy. I feel this surge of energy, and it is a complete arousal state. Instead of expelling the energy outward (like we do with sex or masturbation) I am able to direct the energy inward and upward. My whole body is filled with this energy. Sometimes I can do it intentionally, and other times it just happens. It's overwhelming. I want to have sex with anything, it's really bizarre. On and off for years I've also had the experience of feeling violated in this hyper-aroused lucid dream state. The violation/arousal contrast is confusing and uncomfortable.

To my knowledge I have no sexual trauma in my past (I do have a lot of emotional trauma in my history; my mother was an alcoholic), but that does not necessarily mean I have a completely healthy relationship with sex or this type of energy in general.

---

We can learn to guide our sexual energy in healing and empowering ways. Katie's extremely powerful sexual energy is a gift that she can learn how to use for her own benefit and health. Sometimes, we may find that our sexual energy runs out of control. In yoga, energy centers in the body are called chakras. When the sacral chakra (which is linked to sex and creativity) is unbalanced, this can be flagged up in dreams like Katie's where everything seems sexualized and we want to have sex with anything. To balance the chakras, a regular yoga practice is beneficial.

I suggested that Katie, herself an experienced therapist and dreamworker, write about her feelings of violation to explore them and to see if there is a bridge to her waking life experiences, and that she visualize best-case scenarios of what she could do with her sexual dream energy while feeling safe within the experience. She and I talked about the risk that her fear would lead her to stop lucid dreaming and shut down her sexual energy. I advised her not to let that happen, as this powerful energy is a gift—she just needs to learn how to guide it in healing and empowering ways. Sexual energy can also translate as spiritual energy and lead to mystical experience. In dreams, it can be converted into powerful healing energy, creative energy, or it can be mentally sent out to heal the world.

---

## Katie's insights

Healing my relationship with my own sexual energy or power is something I'm now exploring. I am coming to understand that the sexual energy I experience is very powerful and creative and I have to work with it in a healthy way. I am asking myself questions like, "Is there anywhere in my life where I violate myself?" and "Do I have some personal work to do around healing my relationship with sex or sexual energy?" I'm going to keep educating myself on how to dive into these lucid experiences, now that I have the understanding that you helped me see: that I am safe and I can work with this. My hope is that, with more continued emotional work (through counseling), combined with a grounded yoga/meditation practice, I can help refine this energy and use it for exceptional lucid dream experience. I have started some Kundalini yoga to help me. I now have the awareness that the dream isn't unsafe in and of itself. And that I can and will anchor into myself to take care of myself as I continue to explore these experiences.

---

### How to work with uncomfortable sexual dreams

One woman in her twenties who I worked with dreamed she was a ladybird who had flipped onto its back. Her legs were waving helplessly in the air and her genitals were exposed but she could not manage to get back on her feet. Taking this dream as an example, let's look at ways of working with symbolic sexual dream imagery for insight and self-understanding.

1. **Become the dream image or person.** The dreamer becomes the ladybird and speaks with its voice (see the "Dream Talk technique" on page 38). In doing so, she makes a bridge to her current life situation. She realizes that she feels vulnerable and exposed in her sexual relationship, where her partner appears to hold all the power, making her feel that she cannot stand on her own feet.

2. **Change the dream for the better.** The dreamer re-enters the dream imaginatively. She (as the ladybird) realizes that by rocking her body, she can make it move sideways. Still on her back, she rocks towards a pebble and uses it to help her to flip over so that she is standing on her feet again. This feels so much better! She shakes out her wings and flies away.

3. **Absorb the healing image.** The dreamer sketches the healing dream imagery of the ladybird flying away from her
stuck position. She meditates on this imagery and uses
Lucid Writing to find out more about it. In doing so, she
comes to see that she has more power and resourcefulness
than she gives herself credit for. She is free and can fly away
from her relationship if she wants to, or act to change the
situation for the better and reclaim her own power.

PRACTICE #27

## COLORED BREATHING
## FOR EMOTIONAL SAFETY

If you feel unhappy about the kind of sexual dreams you are
having—if they leave you feeling ashamed, overwhelmed, anxious, or guilty—this cleansing practice can help you to feel safe
and grounded inside your body, not only while you are awake,
but while you are asleep and dreaming. It can help to transform
negative emotions or energies into positive, healing ones.

1. Lie down comfortably with your legs apart and your arms
   slightly away from your body, and close your eyes.
2. Focus on your breath as it moves gently in and out of your
   body. Relax.
3. Picture a color that you love, one that is linked with beauty,
   like sea blue or sunshine yellow. Imagine that every time you
   breathe in, you are breathing this beautiful color right into your
   body.
4. As you breathe steadily in and out, picture this colored breath
   entering your body through your nose and mouth and moving
   down your throat into your tree-like lungs. See it pass through

tiny air sacs into your bloodstream and move all around your body, filling you with a sensation of warmth and safety.

5. Keep seeing your chosen color as it brings healing light and energy into every single part of your body. Breathe it in and imagine your whole body glowing with this color. Breathe and release as the color expands through you, and feel your muscles relaxing, your sense of safety growing.

6. Enjoy being filled with this beautiful color. Save inside you the pleasurable feeling that your color gives you. When you are ready, take one last deep breath in, and release it. Open your eyes.

7. This practice can also be used to incorporate healing dream energy (sexual or otherwise) into the body, by breathing in a highly positive dream image rather than a color. Practices like this one should only ever be done with positive dream imagery!

)———(

# SIX

# Healing from the past
## *supporting your younger self*

Who cares about the past? It's over, right? We can't change it, so why not just skip this chapter and move on?

Except that the past is a vital part of who we are today. Our patterns of thinking and behaving have all grown out of our past, and those old patterns are creating and recreating our lives on a daily basis, even leading us to repeat mistakes or get ourselves into messy situations. The past is not dead: it lives on inside us, whether we are aware of it or not. The wonderful thing is that we can change our relationship to it; and in doing so we dissolve the power that negative past experiences may still have over us.

Healing from the past is one of the central goals of psychotherapy. Dreamwork is an important therapeutic technique within this healing process. When Sigmund Freud's *The Interpretation of Dreams* came out in 1900, dreams were brought to the forefront of psychoanalysis. Although some of Freud's central ideas are highly contested among modern dreamwork professionals, it's largely thanks to him that we in the West woke up to the value of dreams in understanding the self. A century after the publication of Freud's seminal work, in a 2000 paper in the *Journal of Psychotherapy Practice and Research*, Michael Schredl and colleagues reported that the use of dreams in psychotherapy is still an important and frequently used therapeutic technique with high treatment success rates. Dreamwork withstands the test of time.

Psychologists and dreamworkers attest to the importance of releasing powerful feelings and memories that may be holding us back in our lives. Dreams bring these feelings and memories to consciousness so that we can free ourselves from them. Brenda Mallon has been a counselor for nearly forty years. In *Dreams, Counselling and Healing*, she describes how, when people work therapeutically with dreams, they can recognize their anxieties, fears, and relationships with others. Mallon mentions a woman who dreamed of her parents as cardboard cutouts: silent and disinterested. The woman realized the dream was expressing deep feelings from her childhood about the lack of emotional support she'd had from her parents. Once such feelings are brought to consciousness, we can begin to do the healing work of acknowledging and integrating them, and ultimately moving on from them, so that we are freed from the limits they impose on us and the painful emotions associated with them.

As you work through this chapter, please bear in mind that dreams can reveal forgotten memories that are very difficult to accept, such as experiences of sexual abuse or violence. If you are experiencing emotions that are *too extreme and too disturbing* in your dreams, please do not work on them alone. There is never any need to suffer alone, and even though your dreams are fundamentally trying to help you, sometimes they may simply feel too intense for you to handle. If this is the case for you, get in touch with an experienced dreamworker or psychotherapist who can help you to do this work (please see the resources section at the end of this book, pages 199–202).

Healing from the past takes three steps. In this chapter, we'll look at these three steps and how dreams can help us with each one of them.

1. Remember the past.
2. Give your younger self the tools, support, healing, and love he or she needed back then but didn't have.
3. Release the past.

### Remember the past

Looking at these steps, you might wonder why I've even mentioned the first one: remember the past. Surely we can all remember only too well the bad stuff that has happened to us: the stress of our parents divorcing; the struggle to find a satisfying job; or how distraught we were when a family member died. Yet it is astonishing how strongly past trauma can be repressed and held captive by our own unconscious mind to protect us until we are ready to face it.

In a short-story writing course I gave some years ago, the homework was to bring a dream to the next class. The following week, an intelligent, thoughtful man in his late fifties said he never remembered his nighttime dreams, and that all he could recall was one very short dream from his childhood. It was of his grandmother swinging dead from a rope in a barn. I told him this was plenty to work with, and introduced my Lucid Writing technique. After five minutes of writing from their dreams, the group shared what they'd written. When it was the man's turn, he was visibly shocked as he told us what he had discovered as he wrote.

He had realized—after half a century of repressing this information—that his dream was actually a real-life memory. Now flooded with memories, he recalled that when he was eight years old, he had come home to the family farm after school and found his grandmother swinging dead from a rope in the barn: she had hanged herself.

The reaction of his family had been swift and fierce. After the doctor had certified her dead and the body had been taken away, the little boy was sworn to secrecy. The family did not want the shame of the whole village knowing the truth. They decided to tell people that she had died, but not that she had killed herself. The little boy had to suppress this truth. He was not allowed to speak of the trauma of finding his grandmother dead. He was not even allowed to grieve, as her name was now taboo. He was forced to spread a numbing lie over the truth and did this so effectively that he forgot the truth for fifty years!

This may be a particularly extreme example, but forgetting the past, especially highly traumatic events, is not uncommon. Humans can suppress memories of real-life trauma and other bad memories for years on end. When we have suffered, and particularly when we suffered as a child before developing effective coping strategies, the unconscious does us a favour by slamming the lid on that box of memories and too-strong emotions. This amnesia is a protective measure. Years later, the unconscious decides that we are now ready to face whatever it is we repressed. At this stage, the dreams arrive. These may be dreams of wounded children, frightened animals, or even incomprehensible recurring dream images that come arm-in-arm with terrible emotions. Repressed traumas or difficult past emotions come to the surface when we are mature enough and have the necessary coping skills to face them.

Even though the man in my creative writing group recalled the image of his grandmother swinging from a rope, he had dismissed it from his consciousness as nothing more than the remnants of an old nightmare from childhood. Due to the huge lock his unconscious had imposed on that memory, it had been unthinkable for him that it had actually happened. Now that he had acknowledged its reality, he was able to recover true childhood memories and view his family life from a new, aware perspective. After we had talked about this in the group, the man said he felt relieved to know the truth at last, and that many things in his childhood that had never fitted together now suddenly made sense to him. Unlocking that one memory was the first step towards healing his past trauma.

The past can dominate us without us even knowing it. When we connect with our dreams, we open the door to our past. We open the door to healing.

You might think, "If I can't remember certain things from my past, there must be a good reason for it, and frankly, I'd rather not know!" This is absolutely fine: be gentle with yourself and never push anything. The point is not to rake over the past trying to find something to feel upset or aggrieved about. Far from it. This chapter shows what kind of past memories might surface when we begin to work with dreams and how to respond in healing and empowering ways.

## Support your younger self

Back in the late '50s, at mealtimes in my mother's boarding school, the teachers used to put a coat-hanger inside the back of my mother's sweater while she was wearing it so that it scraped on her spine if she slumped, forcing her to sit up straight! It was a technique from a bygone age, and my mother finished boarding school over half a century ago, but guess what—even today, Mum still sits up straight. This is of course not a bad thing, but it serves as an example of how even our posture can be defined by enforced childhood habits.

Throughout childhood, the actions of our parents and other people in our life have a physical, emotional, and spiritual impact that affects who we are today. When we recognize this, we can take steps to release what we no longer need—hang-ups, old hurts, self-criticisms, complexes—and move forward. This is not to say that we should blame our parents, teachers, or even the school bully. They were probably doing the best they could at the time, given their own past and their own level of development.

Blaming the past is pointless and a huge waste of energy.

What we need to do is transform our relationship with, and attitude to, the past. Dreams help us to remember the past, and they help us to heal from it by releasing intense emotions around past events and enabling us to move on. It can also be beneficial to practice affirmations such as the ones below, as these help us to love and accept ourselves as we are today, as well as all of the younger selves we carry within us.

## PRACTICE #28

### AFFIRMATIONS FOR LOVING THE SELF

Choose an affirmation, or make up one of your own. Say these every day while brushing your teeth in front of the bathroom mirror, or any time you have a brief moment to reflect. They are also excellent to use every time you notice a negative or critical thought about yourself. If you think, "I'm such a useless parent," replace that with, "I am doing my best, and I love myself for it." Over time, this thought replacement becomes natural and your self-love and self-respect will increase. When it does, you'll see the benefits in your life as your relationships with others become more harmonious. Here are some affirmations for loving the self.

◊ I love and forgive myself.
◊ I accept myself completely as I am.
◊ It's good to love and care for myself every day.
◊ I am doing my best, and I love myself for it.
◊ I love myself, and others love me.
◊ When I cherish myself, I am better able to cherish others.
◊ There is an abundance of love in the world for everyone, including me.

>———<

## *What is the "inner child?"*

Your inner child is simply your much younger self. We have many younger selves! Inside each of us is the one-year-old us, the two-year-old us, the three-year-old us, and so on, right up to our present-age self. In dreams, we have much easier access to our younger selves than we do when we're awake. Sometimes we may not feel that we are a child in the dream but something will pinpoint our age, such as the age of another person in the dream. When recalling a dream, we might say something like, "In the dream, I was in my childhood home, and I was sixteen," or "In the dream, I was doing that car-washing job I did two summers ago." Or we'll dream of a toddler and say, "And then in the dream, I became the toddler." Dreams are not bound by time or space. When we dream, we become time travelers. We easily transcend time to become a younger self or even an older self.

Many aging people report clear memories of their childhood returning to them at a time when their short-term memory is getting shaky. All of our life memories are stored somewhere inside us. We just don't need them most of the time, or are too busy to think about them, so we close the door on them and forget about them.

In dreams, the door to the past opens.

Through dreamwork, we can give all of our younger selves love and support retrospectively, from our position here and now, with all the knowledge and understanding and strength that we have. By doing this, we heal our past. When we heal the past, we optimize the present, and so create a happier future.

## Inner child dreams

Karen had abandoned her emotional self in her childhood to fit in with her family's expectations that she should be "grown up" and not express her emotions. Forced to shut off from herself in this way, she lost her connection with who she really was, and beneath the outer layer of her life, there was a volcanic build-up. When she began to do intensive inner work with a life coach, her dreams erupted, flowing thick and fast. Since her coach didn't know how to advise her about dreams, Karen approached me. She was having violent, weird, extremely vivid dreams every night, and she found this frightening and emotionally exhausting.

I reassured her that all dreams (no matter how weird!) come to help and heal; it's just a question of understanding the symbolism and allowing the dream story or inner movie to move forward into a happier place. I suggested that the more adept Karen became at that, the clearer her dreams would become, so it was worth bearing with all this crazy outpouring, as it would calm down. Karen shared a series of violent dreams such as the one below, in which she was shooting people.

---

### Karen's dream: Shooting People Dead

*I dreamed that I was surrounded by people and I felt danger. I shot them all several times to make sure they were really dead. Only later in the dream did I become aware that they were all parts of myself.*

What I found very positive in most of Karen's dreams was her dawning awareness *while the dream was actually happening* of what the dream represented. She was clearly aware that she was rejecting certain parts of herself in these dreams—parts she felt so separate from that she viewed them as highly threatening, dangerous enemies whom she needed to kill. These dreams are not fully lucid by any means, but this reflective conscious awareness within the dream highlights Karen's growing consciousness as she understands, even while she is dreaming, what these figures represent. Then a breakthrough dream arrived:

*I dreamed that a child died. I was traumatized and grieved. I remember being at my parents' house and feeling out of control. At the end of the dream I realized it was my inner child and then she came back to life in my arms, and I put her safely under the Christmas tree.*

Karen felt that in this dream she was starting to value and appreciate parts of herself that she had only ever rejected before. In previous dreams, she had killed her inner child.

---

With this evolving dream series, Karen made huge leaps in reintegrating her inner child. Death in dreams often represents a shift, and the fact that her inner child came back to life at the end seemed to reflect her ability to transform her relationship with her own past self, through beginning to care deeply about herself for the first time. It can be traumatic to experience such dreams, but they reflect the dreamer's own brave transformation. Her last dream may be cherished as it contains within it a deeply healing story that can accompany Karen as she keeps working to heal her relationship with her parents and integrate and nurture her younger selves.

It is essential to take care of children and babies in dreams. Save the child if it is in danger. Give it comfort, food, safety. If it is wounded, heal it. If it dies, bring it back to life. If none of this healing work happens in the dream, you can help it to happen by doing Lucid Dreamplay. Your dream children need you. Through dreamwork such as the following practice, we can re-enter the dream and give the child-self in our dream advice or practical help.

PRACTICE #29

## NURTURE YOUR YOUNGER SELF

You can do this using any dream you have had of a child. It doesn't matter if you identified the child in your dream as yourself or not. For the most part, any child that appears in your dreams can be viewed as an aspect of yourself. Alternatively, this exercise can be done by choosing yourself at any age or stage of your life: you could return to a time in your life when you had postnatal depression, or when your father died, or a period when you were feeling lonely. The point of the exercise is to return to a moment in your life when you were in need of help, love, and comfort, and to provide that from your current older, wiser perspective. This is a way of nurturing yourself, of acknowledging the times in your life when you have suffered, and of moving on from those experiences by releasing their emotional charge.

1. Have a pen and paper at hand. Close your eyes and bring up a picture of any dream you've had of a child. Or if you prefer, imagine yourself at a younger age. This might be you as a small child, or at a more recent age.

2. Focus on your younger self (or dream-self) with compassionate attention. Notice any emotions that arise. Delve as deeply as you can: see what is happening in the heart and mind of your younger self. How does he or she feel? Is he or she in trouble of any kind? What is happening—is there any action or movement?

3. Open your eyes very slightly, pick up your pen, and write without stopping to consider your words or correct anything. Write fast to maintain the connection with your unconscious.

4. What you write is entirely without limits. You might find yourself describing any imagery you see, any emotions you feel, or further unpacking a memory from that time in your life. You may find a new, more positive chain of imagery developing in your imagination. If you are working with a dream where a baby or child dies or is hurt, mentally enact helping them, remembering that anything is possible—in this kind of imaginative dreamwork, the dead can be brought to life, and wonders can be worked. You can write from the perspective of your younger self, or write a dialogue between you as you are today and your younger self as she or he was then. Maybe your younger self has questions for you. Find a way of offering solace and guidance.

5. If you like, finish your writing with an affirmation that feels right for this particular younger self. This could be linked to any advice you gave yourself, or it could be more general: "I release the past and feel happiness in my heart."

)————(

One lovely way of reconnecting with your inner child is to do something playful that you enjoyed doing when you were young—go ice-skating again, collect treasures on a country walk, or do free-and-easy artwork, allowing yourself to really have fun with it and make a creative mess. This practice can be done with any dream you like.

## PRACTICE #30

## ART THERAPY FOR YOUR INNER CHILD

1. Collect some basic art tools: paints and brushes, magazines, scissors, glue, modeling clay, and whatever takes your fancy

from outdoors—autumn leaves, fallen pine cones. Purposefully go for things that a kid would love—squirty paints, glitter glue, snail shells.

2. Sit with your eyes closed and re-enter your dream imaginative-ly until it is bright and real. Hone in on the most emotional image of your dream movie and feel that emotion in your heart and body.

3. Open your eyes and without overthinking it, quickly sketch, collage, or mold your dream image. Fully re-experience any emotions from the dream, and let your hands do whatever they like to transmit them. There is no right or wrong, so relax about how your art looks and focus on allowing the energy of your dream to come through. You can be slapdash, playful, or how-ever you want to be. Nobody will judge you on this; it's just a bit of fun. Think of it as a way of engaging with your inner child.

)———(

## Release the past

Releasing the past is the final step in healing. You may ask, "Isn't forgetting something more healing than remembering it and having to relive it?" But repressing something takes a lot of energy and is stressful: repressing our own past could make us ill if we don't find ways of coping with it. Let's look at the cathar-tic process of releasing the past, through this lucid dream that Australian artist Jane had.

### Jane's dream: A Dead Mummy Releasing

I have had problems with digestion for a long, long time. This digestion issue started after the sudden death of my mother twenty-one years ago. I had never properly digested my mother's sudden death and the disintegration of my family just as I was dealing at the same time with a clinically depressed husband and a new baby. I look back now and I realize I was unable to digest the multiple traumas of that time.

*I am examining an unwrapped, mummified body; its torso to mid-thigh region. I notice that the skin is shiny and leathery, an intriguing browny-orange color. I am lucid and think, "This is me. A dead mummy." Then out of its vagina comes a gush of orangey-brown fluid. I revise my dream title in my lucid state. "Correction. 'A Dead Mummy Releasing.'"*

I woke up feeling shaken by the dream. I felt old and somehow desiccated and dried up. I worried that this dream was a harbinger of a desiccated, dry old age. As we worked with the dream, I started to accept that this powerful image was notifying me that I was starting to release the old ideas, emotions, and feelings that had been stuck for so many years.

---

When I met Jane at an IASD conference, despite her feeling desiccated and dried up, my impression was of a vibrant woman, ready to laugh, with a joyous creative energy. I guessed that her energy was already shifting radically postdream, perhaps because the dream was releasing past trauma in the form of stuck energy. I remarked to her that her dream seemed to be not only "a dead mummy releasing," but also "releasing dead Mummy," as Jane finally seemed to have found the time to release all those old feelings after her mother's death, and they seemed ready to turn into a new creative phase.

Jane replied, "Yes! You are absolutely right. What a spot-on insight! And yes, once I'd shared my dream, the stuck dead mummy feeling started to shift. It was probably leftover grief and loss that was coming away and making me feel so terrible. If the trauma of my mother's death has been locked into me for twenty years, of course it's going to be mummified and desiccated. I realize the dream was releasing this energy. I feel like I have totally cracked the code with this dream thanks to your help."

Dreams can help us to ease the pain and emotional angst of the past by releasing it in ways that enable us to move forward in new directions and enjoy our life to the fullest. The mummy in Jane's dream could symbolize transition into a new life, and be a marker of preparation for the next creative baby.

When we release the past, we free up huge amounts of creative energy.

I spoke to Jane six months after we'd worked on her dream, and she was involved in incredibly creative projects: she was directing a live multimedia performance at a festival and had been accepted to do a master's degree in art therapy. She told me, "I am now amazed at your prediction, that once I'd integrated the energy of the dream, it could be the harbinger of a new creative world. The process of unpacking the dream with you was the hard proof I needed to realize that art therapy and dreaming work was the direction that I was always heading to. I am now 100 percent committed to moving forward."

When we let go of the past, we open the door to new opportunities and assure ourselves a happier future.

## Forgiveness

We have looked at how dreams and dreamwork can help us to remember past experiences, support and cherish our younger selves, and release negative past events. The final step in healing from the past is forgiving those who have hurt us. Forgiveness is an absolutely transformative practice. When we truly forgive others for what they did to us and how they made us feel, we create space for new and beautiful experiences to enter our life. Forgiveness can seem to work like magic by healing our relationships and enabling us to move forward in life with a greater sense of self-worth and freedom. Don't worry about how to forgive the person or people who have hurt you; just be willing to forgive them. Release them, and in doing so you'll release the hold the past has over you. You'll become free. Forgiveness alone is enough to change your whole life.

## PRACTICE #31

### FORGIVE—LOVE—RELEASE

Just as important as forgiving others is forgiving ourselves. We can be so hard on ourselves! My Forgive—Love—Release exercise can be used for forgiving others and for forgiving ourselves, so that we can release the past and move into a happier future.

1. Get comfortable, sitting or lying down. Take a couple of slow, deep breaths to clear your mind, and close your eyes.
2. Picture the person you want to forgive. If the mere sight of them invokes strongly negative emotions in you, visualize them as a small child instead.
3. Say, "I forgive you, X, for causing me pain." Really feel yourself forgiving them.
4. Then say, "I send you love, X." Visualize this as golden light illuminating the person.
5. Finally, say, "I release my pain." Breathe out your pain and feel it dissolving. If at any point you find recriminations or negative emotions building up against the person you are trying to forgive, either repeat the steps above, or leave this exercise for today and return to it when you feel ready to.
6. Do this same exercise for yourself. Say, "I forgive myself," and list the things you forgive yourself for. Say, "I love myself," and mean it from the bottom of your heart.

)———(

# SEVEN

# Nightmares and how to resolve them

We've all woken happy and refreshed from a particularly lovely dream, or scared and sad because of a vivid nightmare. The dreams we have color our days; they get us off to a good start or a bad one. Nightmares are upsetting or highly disturbing dreams. Everybody has occasional nightmares, and these can in fact be the best dreams to work with as they are emotionally rich, deep, and often carry a message to help us through life. Dreams want us to heal. And they are prepared to do everything in their power to help us to do so—even plague us with nightmares, if that's what it takes to get our attention. But what if we keep having nightmares? What does this mean, and how can we change the situation for the better?

There are two key things to remember about nightmares:

1. Having the occasional nightmare can be a good thing in the sense that they are often excellent for Mindful Dreaming, illuminating unconscious issues that we need to address and gifting us with deep insights into our lives.
2. Having too many nightmares, or suffering from recurring nightmares, is not good because it disrupts our sleep and can cause serious erosion to our happiness, with some people even becoming scared to go to sleep.

In this chapter, we'll look at how to resolve recurring nightmares and how to work with any kind of nightmare in positive ways, including those caused by trauma. We'll also look at how to liberate ourselves from nightmarish sleep paralysis experiences.

Many people who suffer from chronic nightmares don't recognize how much their nightmares are disturbing their sleep. Sleep is vital for good health, so anything that disturbs it needs to be attended to. Some people have such awful nightmares that they unconsciously delay their bedtime, doing everything they can to avoid sleep, and after a while they wind up with insomnia. Now they have not one problem, but two! This introduces a third, major problem: that of being less able to cope with life's problems because the person is so exhausted. Luckily, there are some easy steps we can take to make sure we have a happier dreamlife and healthy, recuperative sleep.

Nightmares are often seen as simply being caused by stress or caused by trauma. But when we look more closely at the way the brain works, we see that recurrent nightmares are also a learned behaviour. This means that, like a broken record, the brain slips into a groove it recognizes, and nightmares occur again and again. The good news here is that a learned behaviour can be changed. If you have gotten into the bad habit of having nightmares, you can break that habit. It's a simple thing to do, and decades of research spearheaded by psychiatrist Dr. Joseph Neidhardt and sleep disorder specialist Barry Krakow, MD, have shown it to be extremely powerful. They discovered that when you change the nightmare story, you have fewer nightmares and better quality of sleep, resulting in a stronger ability to cope with waking life. Changing the nightmare story jolts the brain out of its negative groove and into a new one.

Lucid dreaming is also an effective technique for combatting nightmares and reducing their frequency. One 2003 study by Victor Spoormaker and colleagues gave participants a one-hour session to talk about the possibilities of becoming lucid in nightmares and changing the dream for the better. They were also given lucid dreaming induction techniques. A follow-up session two months later showed that in all cases, the frequency of nightmares was reduced, and the overall quality of sleep was higher. When we wake up inside a scary dream, we are in a strong position to be able to change the dream, for example by sending love to the frightening dream figure, asking if they have a message for us, or by using lucid "super-powers" to overcome them if this feels necessary. Our understanding that we are dreaming empowers us to act to change the dream in positive, creative ways, and we are less likely to suffer from nightmares. Even if you are not a frequent lucid dreamer, the healing that is available to the lucid dreamer is available to anyone who practices Mindful Dreaming.

## *What to do when dreams turn into nightmares*

Dreams are very happy to talk to us. As soon as you start paying attention to your dreams and begin to write them down, they will become brighter, even more inventive, and respond to your questions. But dreams are not just there for polite chit-chat. Dreams will shout at us in the form of nightmares when there is something our unconscious mind needs us to understand. Whether we are suppressing hidden parts of ourselves, not giving ourselves enough love and care, or if we are hell-bent on a path of self-destruction, dreams act as a mirror, showing us how we are really feeling. We start to have nightmares. Here are some ways of engaging with nightmares to create a happier dreamlife.

PRACTICE #32

## CREATE A HAPPIER DREAMLIFE

1. **Ask the dream a question.** When you become lucid in a nightmare, remind yourself that you can transform this into a learning, healing experience. Take a calming breath and ask the threatening figure or disturbing element of the dream, "What do you want?" or, "Why am I dreaming about this?" "What are you here to teach me?" "Do you have a message for me?" or, "What does this situation symbolize in my life?" The dream scene might spontaneously transform into something else, or you might hear an answer in the form of a disembodied voice.

2. **Send peace and love to whatever is upsetting you.** Send love, peace, forgiveness, or healing white light to the threatening dream figure or situation. Really feel it in your heart. This usually transforms the dream in an instant. You can try either of the above approaches in a waking dream re-entry.

3. **Incubate a healing dream.** Ask your dreams to send you a healing dream to help you to release a past trauma, or to break the cycle of nightmares. Write down your request on a piece of paper and put it under your pillow, touching it whenever you wake in the night to remind yourself of your intention. Write down all your dreams, and look out for healing imagery such as vibrant nature, healthy animals, gorgeous landscapes, or highly positive encounters with dream figures. Absorb your healing imagery whenever you can, using the "Take a healing breath" practice on page 87.

4. **Explore the negative element as "part of myself."** This is a waking technique. Work out which part of the nightmare has the strongest negative emotional charge for you. Is it the leopard prowling through your bedroom? Or the old woman with a

death's-head face? It might be an ominous mountain, or the dizzy sensation you get when you look into a bottomless chasm. Identify the negative emotion in one or two words and then retell the dream from the perspective of that negative part of the dream *as if it is a part of yourself.* For example, the prowling leopard might become "the cruel, dangerous part of me." As you retell the dream, you'll discover what this cruel, dangerous part of you wants and needs, and why.

Try labeling any other negative elements of the dream in the same way, and see how they interact together when you retell the dream story. The results can be illuminating, and people often find that the negative parts of their dream are actually not as negative as they supposed; the leopard may not be cruel and dangerous—you may discover that he feels lost and out of place in your bedroom and wishes he could find his way home. Here, the next step in the dreamplay would be to ask yourself, "Where in my life do I feel lost and out of place?" When we make the bridge to waking life, the dream's meaning often becomes clear.

5. **Embrace the "Shadow."** Nightmares bring us face to face with the creative power of the Shadow archetype. As you'll recall, archetypes are original patterns, mythic characters, or images that emerge from the collective unconscious. The Shadow archetype represents all that we have repressed—the darker side of ourselves. When we choose to be a particular kind of person (for example, sweet-tempered), this automatically implies a choice *not* to be a certain way (in this case, angry). But this doesn't mean that these repressed characteristics disappear: they live on in our unconscious. These rejected aspects of the self can surface in nightmares. We might dream of angry people, or of reacting angrily ourselves. Then we wake up and think, "I would never have got so angry in waking life!" This is a clue that the dream is revealing a shadow aspect of the self; something we're suppressing.

Jung believed that it is important to embrace the Shadow whenever we meet it, in order to have a whole, healthy psyche. He felt that the Shadow is the source of creativity and brings great gifts to the psyche, but we can only receive these gifts by facing the Shadow and accepting it. Nightmares show us rejected aspects of ourselves that we need to integrate. Becoming lucid in a nightmare, or doing Lucid Dreamplay after the dream, can be very effective for integrating the Shadow and so benefiting from its gifts. When we embrace our Shadow, we grow happier and more balanced.

)———(

When we pay attention to our nightmares and attempt to act on their message, they begin to change into healing dreams, as happened for Susan. She was plagued by a recurring nightmare of being trapped and became scared to sleep in case it happened again.

### Susan's dream: Trapped

*In my dream I was asleep and then woke up in the middle of the night and felt like I needed to get out of the bedroom urgently, only there was no door. I felt like I was actually awake but I clearly wasn't. I was really disoriented, didn't even know which way was up and which way was down. Eventually I woke up and felt very scared and dazed.*

Each time the dream repeated itself, it was more intense. Until Clare told me that dreams come to help us and that I should write them down, I never knew that dreams had a purpose. I didn't know there was a science of dreaming. Once you know there's a system, you can make sense of it. I wasn't going to bed scared any more because I knew the dreams were helping me.

I started to keep a dream journal. I also began to address past issues and accept past feelings rather than trying to push them away. The nightmare made me feel trapped, and I wanted to get out but in reality I think that it wasn't so much wanting to get out as wanting to get in touch with a part of me I'd lost touch with. Soon afterwards, I experienced a shift, where the nightmare spontaneously changed into something wonderful.

*I dreamed I was asleep and again I woke up and felt this urgent need to get out of the room, only it wasn't my room this time. In my dream I got up, expecting not to find a door, but the door was there and it was open and I went outside and was in a beautiful garden.*

---

Susan did three important things to cause the shift in her nightmares. Firstly, she accepted the idea that her dreams come to help her, which made her less scared of going to sleep. Secondly, she started keeping a dream journal, which is a vital way of building a relationship with dreams. Thirdly, she stopped suppressing past feelings and began to address them. On all three levels, Susan's new attitude enabled an opening up to her unconscious mind. She began to listen, and was rewarded with a way out of her recurring nightmares (symbolized by the door) and into the growing beauty of her own being, symbolized by the garden in her dream.

PRACTICE #33

## HOW TO TRANSFORM NIGHTMARES

Lucidity, whether it is dream lucidity or the waking lucidity we experience when we work with a dream while awake, has such long-lasting effects on nightmares because we realize *we can change the situation*. When we are able to face our inner demons in a nightmare, we reap the benefits. This realization can empower dreamers to transform their nightmares for good. However, some nightmares are too strong to face alone. Please avoid these techniques if you are clinically depressed, suicidal, suffering from psychotic episodes, or if you have severe anxiety disorder or have recently lost a loved one. In these cases, it is better to seek out a trained therapist who can give you personalized guidance on how to handle your nightmares.

1. Any time after you wake up, re-enter your nightmare imaginatively by allowing the images and events of the dream to flood your mind. Remember that you are perfectly safe. Watch the flow of imagery and emotions as if you are watching a movie. Notice any symbolism, possible meanings, or connections to your waking life, without forcing associations.

2. As your dream movie flows along, identify the moment when the dream changes into a nightmare. Look for the moment when your heart starts pounding in fear, or the bad man appears in the street. When you identify this moment, you know where the dreamwork might usefully begin, and you can work to restore balance.

3. Rewind your dream to any point that feels right for you. Now imagine that you are lucid in this dream: you know that you are dreaming and you are free to change the action in any way you wish. You have the power of flight, invisibility, and immortality. You can call for help and it will appear, you can ask the scary man why he is chasing you, or find out what the dead baby under the table symbolizes. Know that this is your dream and that you can recreate it in your imagination in positive, healing ways.

4. Be spontaneous and decide in the moment how to respond, safe in the knowledge that you are guiding this process and can stop it any time you like. Sometimes simply reliving the nightmare without fear, making no effort to change the action, pro-

vides all the insight and healing we need. You can replay the dream several times, experimenting with different possible solutions until you hit on the right one. When you do, you'll know it: your tension around the dream images will lessen and you'll feel a lot better.

>———<

This technique can help us to understand the message of an upsetting dream so that we can transform and heal. Let's have a look at the following scary dream I had a few years ago, to see how I worked to transform and learn from it.

## Clare's dream: The Toilet-Woman Nightmare

*I'm in a large public building. I enter a toilet cubicle, but someone else is in there. To my shock, I see it is a woman who is sitting on the toilet but has been completely squashed by the lid. She is bent double, her face forced down into the toilet bowl and her arms trailing at her sides. Her long blonde hair hangs down to the ground and she is very still.*

*She has drowned in the toilet.*

*Quickly, I back out and dart into the next cubicle, my heart beating very fast. The scene is so shocking that I become lucid. I recognize that I feel very reluctant to go back and face this terrible dream image. Before I can do anything, I wake up with an unpleasant jolt.*

This dream came along one winter shortly after my five-year-old daughter had been diagnosed with a serious disease. Doctors had prescribed treatment, but despite all our efforts, Yasmin's health was not improving and we had just been told that her bronchitis had worsened and she was on the cusp of getting pneumonia again. My dreams had been rumbling warnings to tell me that I was under stress and upset by the situation. I had dreamed of flooded grey fields; a caged orangutan with anguished eyes; and even had a dream where I thought, "I am undergoing pain!" I wrote these dreams down and knew I needed to work with them. But the day-to-day reality of caring full-time for a sick little child took over everything.

When this nightmare came along, I was particularly struck by the fact that *even when I became lucid in the dream, I didn't want to face the terrible dream image*. I've had many thousands of lucid dreams and I'm usually brave about facing difficult imagery in them, so this telling hesitation showed me just how strong the dream image was. I simply had to face it and find out what it wanted me to know. I closed my eyes, relaxed, and mentally went back into my dream. Here's what happened:

*I re-enter the dream as an observer and watch my shocked dreaming self as she walks in on the woman trapped by the toilet seat. I put my arm around my dreaming self to support her. Then, spontaneously, I become her. I lift the toilet seat and get the woman out. I lay her out on the floor. She seems cold and lifeless, but I rub some cream onto her cold neck and under her ears and throat, even over her lips. This reactivates her circulation and she "comes back to life."*

*I realize she hasn't died; only fainted.*

*I rub down her arms and hands. The woman moves and sits up, and I hug her. I help her to her feet and notice that there is a piece of jewelry—a ring—inside the toilet bowl. I pick it out and wash both it and my hands in the sink before giving it back to the woman. She had lost it down the toilet and had been looking for it when she lost consciousness.*

*I ask her if she wants to leave the cubicle and she says yes. We go out of the building and cross the road to get into a green park. In the park I look at the woman's ring. It is bright blue and beautiful. I ask her what it means to her. She answers simply, "Hope."*

*I think, "Oh! She lost her hope down the toilet!"*

Suddenly the meaning of my dream is clear: during the difficult weeks following Yasmin's diagnosis, part of me had lost hope and had almost drowned or got trapped or shut down from the loss of hope. Now I have rescued the part of me that felt trapped, and recovered my hope.

---

This realization felt huge: finally I was accepting the toll that the past months had taken on me instead of pushing my feelings into the background. I felt that helping the toilet woman and recovering the ring was a very healing, supportive act. The symbolism of washing the ring to restore it felt purifying. In one short bit of dreamwork, I had identified the meaning of my nightmare, embraced this shadow side of myself, and changed the outcome of my dream. I kept the healing image of the ring with me to remind me of the power of hope as the days passed and my daughter's health gradually improved. Thankfully, she didn't get pneumonia on that occasion and as the winter turned into spring, she grew much stronger.

It can be hard for anyone to acknowledge the hopeless, trapped part of myself. Who wants to admit the existence of a defeated, uninspiring, shadow part of the self? I'd rather soldier on being Supermum, always ready with a smile and a hug for my child, able to cope in any situation. But we are all fragile: it's easy to get broken if we ignore what's really going on inside us. Dreams don't lie. "Look," they say, "this is how you're truly feeling: as if you've drowned in a toilet. It's not good, and it's not healthy. Sort it out!"

The transformation of my nightmare took under ten minutes but its impact was huge. Mindful Dreaming doesn't need to be a long, drawn-out process; just a few minutes can be beneficial. As soon as I had resolved this nightmare, my nightly dreams burst forth with healing imagery. In one dream, I climbed up from a dark cellar into light and air, and in another, I was sitting high up in a lifeguard's chair on a sandy beach in the sunshine, watching the sheer beauty of the waves rolling in while I thought, "I am totally relaxed and happy!" My dreamlife reflected the usefulness of the Mindful Dreaming I had done: instead of trying to flush my unwanted, unacknowledged feelings of hopelessness down the toilet, I had accepted those feelings and healed that part of myself. In doing so, I had transformed into the happy lifeguard; a mother who was able to appreciate the sheer beauty of life while safeguarding her child's life.

You can use your imagination to transform any nightmare you experience. Equip your dreaming self with special powers, strong allies, and inner resources. Do whatever feels right to support and help your dreaming self. If you like drawing, sketch your favorite nightmare solutions. Remind yourself, "I am a strong, resourceful dreamer." The more you play around creating possible solutions to your nightmares, the more deeply ingrained this habit will become, and you'll find it spilling over into your dreamlife in recognizable ways: you'll become braver, more creative and resourceful in your dreams, and your dreamlife will improve beyond measure.

## Mindful Dreaming to heal from trauma-induced nightmares

When someone has been through a trauma, they are likely to have disturbing dreams about it. The root cause might be anything from sexual abuse to torture; from a dreadful car accident to the experience of fighting in a war. In these nightmares, the root trauma is often replayed and the sufferer wakes up in a state of extreme stress. According to the National Center for PTSD in the US, research has established that when trauma survivors have posttraumatic stress disorder (PTSD), 71–96 percent of them may suffer from nightmares, and some of them have nightmares several times a week. About half of trauma-related nightmares are a direct replay of the traumatic event: if someone had been in a hurricane, she might dream of floodwaters and high winds. The best-known therapy for PTSD nightmares was developed in 1995 by Dr. Neidhardt and Barry Krakow, MD. Here are the steps.

## PRACTICE #34

## IMAGERY REHEARSAL THERAPY

1. Write down your nightmare.
2. In your mind, make up a new, positive ending to the nightmare.
3. Mentally rehearse this new ending every day to retrain the mind. Paint a vivid inner picture of the altered version.

)———————(

When we work with healing imagery by changing the nightmare story, we retrain the mind so that it stops slipping into a repeated negative loop in our dreams. In doing so, we have more refreshing sleep and can face the day with stronger energy and resilience. By improving our dreamlife, Mindful Dreaming improves our waking life, too.

Nightmares can be red flags for unresolved trauma. Most of us have experienced trauma in some form. Perhaps we were bullied at school, lost a parent, or witnessed something awful. Trauma can range from seemingly undramatic events such as moving away from a beloved friend when we were young, to horrific events such as being attacked or involved in a serious accident. Dreams can help us to integrate and ultimately release these events when we know how to work with them gently and respectfully.

If we truly manage to release past traumas—which means learning to become less attached to them, and releasing the emotions of fear, guilt, loss, or disgust we have around them—then we can free ourselves from their heavy influence. This allows us to let go of unhelpful emotional patterns such as the habit of feeling unable to act to protect ourselves, or bottling up feelings. It is a vital first step to living a happier life.

Changing the dream story can help us to heal from nightmares, even those associated with deep-rooted traumas. It is also good to purposefully release traumatic memories or disturbing dream imagery, as in the practice below.

## PRACTICE #35

### THE TRAUMA-RELEASING RITUAL

Carry out a ritual to release trauma and upsetting nightmare images. This can be done while either awake or asleep, but if you want to do it in a lucid dream, plan the sort of ritual you'd like to carry out. We all have things in our life that we are trying to let go of—a broken heart; a traumatic memory; guilt; the loss of someone precious. But sometimes letting go can be very hard. Creating a ritual to release what we need to release in order to move forward can be helpful.

1. Keep it simple. Choose an item that symbolizes what you want to release.
2. Decide how you want to release your item. You might choose to place a flower next to ocean waves and watch the tide take it. You may want to ritually destroy your item, or bury it. You might prefer to go to a place of natural beauty and feel the earth holding you and your pain.
3. As you perform your ritual, be aware of the cycle of life and death and rebirth, and be mindful of the eternal here and now of the present moment. Know that you can change and heal.

4. Breathe new air into your lungs and release what you came here to release, one breath at a time.

5. Always give yourself a comforting treat after completing a releasing ritual: a scented bath; your favorite meal; a spa treatment. Take good care of yourself.

)———————(

## Sleep paralysis: how to transform unpleasant presleep sensations into lucid dreams

One stage we all go through as we begin to sleep is known as sleep paralysis (SP). The muscles in our body naturally become paralyzed every single night to stop us from acting out our dreams. This keeps both our bed-partner and us safe from the winning goal we kick during a game of dream football, or the dream aggressor we karate-chop out of town. The only muscles that are not paralyzed are the respiratory muscles (so that we can still breathe) and the eye muscles, which is why you'll sometimes see your partner's eyes moving to and fro under their closed lids when they are asleep.

Most people don't even notice this first stage of sleep as they are not lucidly aware, so they miss it. But what can happen is that people stay conscious as they fall asleep, yet think they are still awake. When they hear strange noises or see weird images (all a natural part of the presleep show we are treated to every night), they panic and try to move, but can't. This can give rise to the extremely unpleasant experience of feeling trapped in your body, unable to control your limbs, with the feeling that there is something nasty close by.

People who suffer from SP often report believing that a menacing intruder is in their bedroom—they can hear his hoarse breathing close to their face. In fact, they are alone in their bedroom and what they can hear is their own breathing. As with so many things, once we know what sleep paralysis is, we find ourselves in a much stronger position to react calmly to all the strange sensations that occur. As well as sensing an intruder, we may also sense dropping off the edge of something; vibrations; feelings of shooting along at great speed; floating; flipping over—along with sounds like buzzing, voices, clicks, and whirrs. I call these odd experiences and sensations The Transition Effect, as they arise when we transition from a waking state to a sleeping state.

The thing to remember about most dream-related experiences is that *any bodily sensation will be instantly translated into vivid imagery.* This is simply how the dreaming mind works: it picks up physiological stimuli such as the need to cough, or a headache, and translates it into "Someone is trying to choke me," or "There's a tight metal band on my head." We hold fear in the body, too, so when the dreaming mind registers shallow breathing and tightly knotted stomach muscles, these will also be changed into vivid hallucinations such as a monstrous being squatting on our chest. In SP, these hallucinations can feel devastatingly real, but they are not real in the objective sense: there is no intruder breathing close to our face; no ghost trying to strangle us in our sleep; no incubus sitting on top of us. All we need to do is calm right down and remind ourselves that we are having a sleep paralysis episode and will wake up safely from this experience.

In SP, you may also have an out-of-body experience (OBE), where you feel that you float or shoot out of your physical body. Understandably, this may feel scary at first. But we all leave our body every night as we transition into a dream body; it's just that we normally don't notice the transition, so there is no reason to fear such experiences. In fact, they provide a great opportunity for a healing or spiritual experience. You may also fall into what many people call "the black void": a dream space of what feels like infinite blackness. Again, this may feel weird at first, but once you know more about this state, you can feel perfectly safe here and use it as a meditative, healing space.

The wonderful thing is, we can use sleep paralysis as a platform to enter a lucid dream. Once we are calm, we can carry our lucid awareness through into a happy dream scenario. Here, the power of visualization is important: you could imagine a hammock swinging between two palm trees on a sandy beach, and step into that scene. Or you could recall some healing dream imagery and breathe it into your body.

Yes, Lucid Dreamplay can be done even when you are stuck in sleep paralysis! This is a highly beneficial time to use healing imagery, as it can instantly free you from a deeply unpleasant experience and lead you directly into a lucid dream.

## PRACTICE #36

## HOW TO TURN SCARY SLEEP PARALYSIS INTO A LUCID DREAM

If ever you have super-real, spooky sensations in sleep paralysis, remember the golden rule of dreaming: *dream images respond directly to your thoughts and emotions.* If you are scared, they tend to get a lot scarier. If you are relaxed, things will calm down. Don't struggle and fight against the paralysis; this rarely has any useful effect and will simply add to your panic. We have control over three things in sleep paralysis: our breathing, our eye movements, and our mental attitude. Learn to calm down by taking a deep breath, consciously relaxing, and reminding yourself, "I am safe in this experience, and I will wake up safely in my bed." Once you feel calmer, you can choose from one of the five actions below, or try a combination of them.

1. Breathing calmly, visualize an egg of white light all around you and allow this "light shield" to protect you.
2. Radiate love and light: use the "Love and Light transformative technique" on page 147 and watch the imagery or unpleasant sensations transform for the better.
3. Imagine a wonderful scene, like floating down a blue river in a wooden boat, or enjoying the view from a mountain top. Focus on this until you can really see it, then allow it to become three-dimensional and step (or fly) into it. Congratulations, you have created your own lucid dream to enjoy!
4. Use the "Take a healing breath" practice on page 87 to breathe your own powerful healing dream imagery into your body. Focus on this imagery and allow it to grow bigger, until it takes up your entire field of vision. Allow it to solidify around you while you remain lucidly aware.
5. Alternatively, you can surrender fearlessly to the sleep paralysis experience. This often leads to a tumble into the lucid black void; a space of nothingness and everythingness, where you can relax and enjoy being bodiless in endless dream space. This is an acquired taste at first, but it can be a gateway to profound spiritual experiences, which we explore in chapter 10.

⟩———⟨

In my early twenties, I used to have almost nightly experiences of sleep paralysis and "black void" dreams where I would float in endless space. It took a huge effort of will not to feel lost and frightened in these experiences at first, as I had no idea what was going on. I trained myself to relax and breathe slowly and deeply, calming my emotions and my mind. The experiences continued, but now I was curious rather than fearful, and I began to notice that the blackness was not just black: it had light in it, sparkling dots like stars, areas of deep color, or sweeping lines of light. I realized it was a fascinating place to be. On a recent fall through the black void, as I fell deeper and deeper into dream space I noticed horizontal streaks of light appearing from time to time; bright ribbons of clear light cutting through the blackness.

All darkness has light within it: be patient and unafraid, and you'll find it.

# EIGHT

# Illness and pain
## *how to dream yourself well*

Imagine a time when there were dream temples throughout the ancient world. Sick people would travel to these temples from far and wide to seek the wisdom of dreams. In Greece, within the ritualized setting of the famous Temple of Asclepius, people would incubate healing dreams to give them insight into how to relieve their ailments. Around 460–380 BC, Hippocrates, the father of modern medicine, taught the therapeutic power of dreams and the importance of dream incubation. Aristotle believed that doctors could diagnose illness by listening to people's dreams, since dreams reflect bodily health.

Today, psychoanalysts, psychologists, and dream researchers recognize the ways in which dreams communicate with us about our health. Dreams can be transparent when it comes to illness and pain. Clinical psychologist Dr. Patricia Garfield reports that following a hysterectomy, one woman dreamed she was brutally raped, reflecting the rough penetration and pain of the operation. Dream therapist Brenda Mallon reports the case of a woman who dreamed she saw a living X-ray of her head that pinpointed the site of a tumor on the base of her brain. She acted fast, the tumor was discovered in that exact spot, and was treated successfully.

Nothing is separate, and our bodies demonstrate the ingenious interconnectedness of systems. Just as our dreams can communicate with us about the state of our health, so too can our mind send powerful messages to our bodies that influence our health. The brain, nervous system, and immune system impact on each other, as shown by findings from psychoneuro-immunology (PNI), a branch of medicine that studies the effect of the mind and psychological processes on health. Our psychological state can render us either more or less susceptible to disease and influence our resistance to illness. Depressed people are more likely to become ill as their low mood affects their immune system. When we support our overall psychological state, we support better health.

Internationally known Austrian sleep disorder specialist Ernest Hartmann suggests that dreaming is critical for good mental and emotional health, and for optimal neurophysiological functioning. Dreams and the body are inextricably linked. When we work with dreams in therapeutic ways, we gradually become happier and feel more whole, giving our bodies a chance to grow stronger. Dreaming is good for our health!

In the first half of this chapter, we'll look at how dreams can warn of illness in the body and how to listen to our dreams to learn more about our health. In the second half, we'll explore how Mindful Dreaming can help us to dream ourselves well.

### Dreams can warn of illness

In his 2015 study, "Warning Dreams Preceding the Diagnosis of Breast Cancer: A Survey of the most Important Characteristics," Dr. Larry Burk found that 94 percent of warning dreams had a sense of urgency and the strong feeling that this was an important dream. Eighty-three percent were more real and intense than usual, 72 percent had a sense of menace or dread, 44 percent used the word "cancer" or "tumor," and in 39 percent there was physical contact with the breast in the dream. Sometimes dreams can be incredibly concrete and specific, but often they employ symbolic language. Dreams are in close communication with the physical body and can provide remarkably specific information about disease. Let's look at three of the warning dreams gathered by Dr. Burk to see how dreams talk to us about disease in the body.

Diana, a cardiac physiologist, dreamed that a female surgeon was operating on her to remove a breast cancer. When she subsequently had a mammogram, there was nothing to be seen, and the doctor refused to do an ultrasound. Diana pointed to the exact spot she had seen in her dream and refused to leave until the doctor did the ultrasound. He found a small cancer tumor and turned white, asking her, "How did you know?" She replied, "I dreamed about it." Soon, her dream came true—her breast cancer was removed by a female surgeon.

Kat O'Keefe-Kanavos found that her dreams would freeze like a computer screen. A dream guide placed Kat's hand on her right breast and told her, "You have cancer right here. Feel it? Go back to your doctor tomorrow." She did, and her cancer was found and treated. Ten years later, Kat is still alive and well. When dreams behave in unusual ways, stopping in midflow or getting interrupted by dream figures, it may indicate that important unconscious knowledge is being pushed towards the dreamer.

Wanda Burch dreamed that her dead father shouted at her in a dream, "You have breast cancer!" Her doctor couldn't find any cancer until Wanda put a dot far under her left breast to show him where to insert the biopsy needle. She knew where the cancer was because she'd had a second, follow-up dream where the debris or tumor had appeared, hidden under a ledge. The surgical biopsy showed that Wanda had an extremely aggressive, fast-moving cancer whose cells were amassing in a way that did not allow them to be seen on a mammogram. Wanda's dreams reveal how familiar figures, dead or alive, can show up to offer advice or warnings and how dreams often come in a series, with each dream providing more information about the disease.

How do dreams know that there is a tiny cancerous tumor growing inside our body? The unconscious mind probably picks up on very subtle physiological signals that something is wrong in a particular area of the body, and dreams automatically turn these signals into messages or symbolic imagery. When we pay attention to our dreams, we may be able to pick up on these early health messages in time to prevent serious illness or even death. It seems that the simple act of writing down our dreams could one day save our life. Yet another incentive to keep a dream journal!

## Ask the dream about your health

We can always incubate a dream about our current health situation to find out more about it. In 2017, doctoral research by Bhaskar Banerji at Saybrook University in the US investigated the links between nocturnal dreams and chronic illness. The participants in Banerji's study listened to a recording every other night to incubate a prescription dream regarding their health condition. One woman in her mid-sixties suffering from chronic liver pain had a dream where a doctor appeared and advised her to stop taking the antihistamines she was using to control her allergies. She followed the dream prescription and a couple of weeks later her liver pain disappeared. We can get specific health advice from our dreams by incubating a healing dream. However, it's best to think of dream-inspired health guidance as complementary to conventional medical care, rather than a replacement for it, so please do always check with your doctor before making any changes to your medication.

Another of Banerji's participants, who suffered from high blood pressure, dreamed of a medical figure who informed her that she was dehydrated and needed to drink more water. She also had many dreams where potatoes made an appearance. She found herself eating potato dishes, serving potatoes; even entering potatoes into a database. She modified her diet to include more water and more spuds, with the result that her blood pressure is now almost normal and she can manage her condition without resorting to medication.

Separately from Banerji's study, Svitlana, a woman I met at an IASD dream conference, incubated a dream to show her what her biggest health problem was. She had the following lucid dream, which took on nightmarish qualities.

## Svitlana's dream: The Alien

*I find myself lucid in a grey zone. It is heavy and gloomy . . . but then something animate emerges from the area of my stomach! It jumps out of me like an alien in the* Alien *films. It looks like a demon. It is a part of me. It is grey, threatening, and horrid. It jumps out of me and twists around and jumps into my face. I get scared and wake up.*

A sensation of fright, danger, and hopelessness stayed with me when I woke up. Everything that was connected to this dream was unpleasant and alarming. Was I supposed to see that thing? Was it an answer to my question about what my biggest health problem is? In the morning, it occurred to me that it was a representation of the immune disorder that I have. Immunity is located in the gut.

This dream did not go away, and the fact that it happened bothered me. I did not share it with anyone. During the IASD dream conference, Clare gave us a task: turn a nightmare into a healing dream by allowing the imagery to transform spontaneously into something healing, or by sending it golden light.

I worked on my threatening dream. In the beginning I did not quite know what to do. Should I get rid of it? Cast the demon out? Cleanse myself of its presence? I first thought of extracting it as a cancerous growth. Yet since it was a part of me, I could not just get it out and dump it. I rejected the cleansing path.

I started getting universal healing golden energy and sending it to the alien. As I infused it with golden energy, it started turning from grey to golden. I gradually turned the alien into a ball of light which was located right below my ribcage. Buzzing with golden energy, the ball became my energetic center, a battery that gave my entire body energy. I thought about the gut as the second brain. I felt that the alien who popped up from my gut was the brain of my immune disorder (rheumatoid arthritis). Wasn't its location, as well as its power to frighten me, indicative of that? But I dealt with it and the warm feeling in my gut lingered. Now it turned into the source of energy and joy.

Right after this invigorating experience I wondered, "Will I need to repeat this healing session?" At this time, I don't feel any need for that.

This dream was especially disturbing because it was a lucid dream. I have never had lucid nightmares before. For me, cracking this dream was the single most important event at the entire conference!

---

When we ask a dream a question about our health, we need to be prepared for an honest answer that might shock and frighten us. The beauty of Lucid Dreamplay is that even the most unhealthy dream images can be transformed into healing dreams. When Svitlana filled her alien with healing golden light, she not only intuitively understood its connection to her rheumatoid arthritis; she also transformed it into something positive and created an empowering source of energy and joy to tap into whenever she needs to. But how can we tell when a dream image relates specifically to our health? Let's look at how to spot health metaphors in dreams.

PRACTICE #37

## HOW TO IDENTIFY HEALTH METAPHORS IN DREAMS

Dreams can be incredibly symbolic, but sometimes they have a very direct message for us: Drink less. Get a massage. Quit smoking. Move your body! It's useful to be able to identify health metaphors in dreams, and the key to this is working closely with your dream journal. Dreams may be commenting on your state of mind or on the state of your body, or both. The more you work with your dream journal, the easier it will become to identify a dream with unhealthy imagery, or one that has a message about your health. You will start to see patterns and themes in your dreams. Often dreams arrive in a sequence, with each dream clarifying further. Color-code or number dreams that seem linked by a particular theme, then keep an eye on how they develop.

1. Go through your dream journal highlighting any references to body parts, vehicles, or buildings. Houses and other structures can represent the body in dreams, so pay attention to their condition: are they shabby or in tip-top condition? Are the foundations solid? Cars and other forms of transport can symbolize the body as the "vehicle" we travel in through life. Notice how the vehicle is functioning: if the brakes aren't working, this could be a metaphor for needing to slow down in life. Is the vehicle heading for an accident, or is everything running smoothly?

2. Highlight emotions that seem particularly strong, negative, or unusual for you and watch to see if they crop up again in other dreams.

3. Put an asterisk next to dream scenes that involve wounds, war, attacks, or unpleasant dream imagery such as maimed animals, broken objects or equipment, dirty water, or sensations such as burning, choking, or pain. Scenes of attack or war may reflect your emotional state but they could also point towards some sort of battle within the body, as it fights off illness. Many people dream of injured animals or destruction before or after having surgery. Scenes of dirty water or broken plumbing may symbolize the kidneys and bladder.

4. Note any direct advice from people in your dreams, no matter how cryptic it seems. Return to this advice now and then to see

if it begins to make more sense in the context of health and your body. A subsequent dream may well clarify it.

5. Ask for a clarifying dream if a particular dream seems important but you can't understand it: simply write the question you want to ask in your dream journal, and repeat it mentally as you fall asleep. Bear in mind that not all bad dreams are predictive of illness! Many simply reflect your emotional state. Rather than panicking, do Lucid Dreamplay to discover more.

)————(

Let's look at how lucid dreaming and various Lucid Dreamplay techniques can help us to improve our health.

## Mindful Dreaming as a healing tool

Positive mental imagery is a powerful aid to healing: one scientific study on the effectiveness of mental imagery in the healing process of over five hundred children and adolescents showed that patients who were taught to use mental imagery reported a greater capacity for healing from a range of health issues, including acute and chronic pain, asthma, and obesity. Fifty-one percent achieved complete resolution of their health issue, while a further 32 percent showed significant improvement.

Dreams are an incredibly vivid type of mental imagery. When we integrate healing imagery from our dreams into our healing process as shown in the practices throughout this book, we are boosting our chances of resolving pain and recovering more quickly from illness. Our personal dream imagery is an especially effective mental tool for healing as we resonate with it emotionally. But what do we do if our dreams are filled with unhealthy imagery? Easy—we use the "Love and Light transformative technique" below. This technique can be used either while actually in the dream or after the dream.

## PRACTICE #38

## LOVE AND LIGHT
## TRANSFORMATIVE TECHNIQUE

Some dream imagery can be identified as unhealthy if it triggers emotions like disgust, fear, or dread, or has elements of decay, attack, wounds, or sickness. If you are ever faced with unhealthy imagery in a dream, such as "Poisonous liquid flows down a mountainside, destroying everything it touches," or "A diseased rat scuttles into my house," you can transform it simply by creating a feeling of love in your heart and sending it towards whatever is upsetting you. This is such a beneficial practice that it's good to practice it in everyday life whenever you get the chance. It can also be used to help heal physical ailments and illness: summon love by following steps 1–3 and direct this love towards the part of your body that is suffering.

1. Take a deep breath and summon a feeling of love. If this seems hard to do, think about someone you love in an uncomplicated way—your baby nephew, your child, your dog.
2. Focus on this warm, expansive feeling of love and imagine it radiating from the center of your heart. Visualize it as a glowing light. The more you practice this technique, the easier it will be to generate love when you're in a bad dream facing something unpleasant. You may find yourself automatically sending love even in nonlucid dreams as the reaction becomes normal for you.
3. Send love. Imagine your radiant love extending outwards to whomever or whatever feels harmful, negative, or upsetting in the dream. See this as a luminous flow of light that encompasses them. Know that this loving light will transform them.
4. Dream imagery is highly responsive to the dreamer's emotions and expectations, so if you get scared in a dream, the imagery

is likely to get scarier in response. If you focus on staying calm and creating a positive emotion like peace, love, healing, or compassion, you are much more likely to calm the imagery and understand its message. This usually results in the spontaneous, positive transformation of the imagery. The poisonous flow of liquid down the mountain might turn into a spread of blossoming flowers that leaves a vibrant meadow in its wake. The diseased rat heals and runs out into the garden to play. Changing the imagery of your inner movie is psychologically healthy as it can help you to resolve conflicts and see that positive change is possible. But the change is powerful only if it feels natural and spontaneous and is fully felt as an emotional event.

5. If you become lucid in a dream, you can also directly ask the imagery, "Do you have a message for me?" or, "What do I need to know?"

6. After a disturbing or distressing dream, do Lucid Dreamplay to create something healing from the experience. Close your eyes, breathe calmly, summon the unhealthy dream image, and send it love or healing golden light. Watch it transform.

>———<

When we grow practiced at summoning love, it can become an automatic response to do this in any situation. When we become lucid in a dream, we can send love to our aggressor or to any negative imagery there is in the dream. The "Love and Light" technique is not only useful for unhealthy dream imagery and nightmares. It is also a valuable waking life practice that can help us to react calmly and compassionately to aggravating people and events. Try it as an experiment the next time your boss speaks to you harshly, or your spouse drives you crazy. Summon love in your heart and send it to them! Watch the situation diffuse.

The highly personal healing imagery we can access through our dreams can help to relieve physical pain. In lucid dreams, we are in immediate contact with healing imagery, and we can use this to help us to heal. In addition to taking medical advice and following conventional treatments, why not use our inner resources to heal ourselves? We all dream every night. This means that every night we have the opportunity to optimize healing in our bodies. The following practice can also be carried out while awake, as Lucid Dreamplay. Just close your eyes, summon the dream in all its sensory glory, and let your imagination and your unconscious do the rest!

PRACTICE #39

## LUCID DREAM HEALING
## OF PHYSICAL ILLNESS AND PAIN

1. When you become lucid, send healing energy to the area of your body that needs it. This can be in the form of a beam of light from your hand, or you might simply place your hand on your body. Affirmations are helpful to focus your healing intent—"I am in radiant health"—or, more specifically, "My knee joint is flexible and pain free."

2. Ask the dream, "Why do I have this illness? Does it carry a message for me?" Or ask, "What must I do to free myself from pain?" Be open to whatever comes, and if nothing happens, rephrase your question and ask again.

3. Summon the healing people in your life: doctors, therapists, warm-hearted friends, or ancestors who have passed away. Ask them to help you to heal.

4. Create a healing environment in the dream, such as a healing hot spring. Lower yourself into it and feel it healing every pore of your skin, every nerve, every cell.

5. Be flexible in the lucid dream. After asking for healing, allow dream events to unfold without controlling them. This way, you

stand to learn a lot more about your health situation, and your unconscious is free to come up with the most creative healing solution.

>————————(

## Spontaneous healing dreams

Sometimes healing dreams arise spontaneously to help us with a specific health situation. Sheila Asato, award-winning artist and director of Monkey Bridge Arts, suffered from chronic pain for years. She had severe endometriosis and her doctors had recommended a complete hysterectomy. Instead, she chose to take an integrative approach to healing that included sessions with a massage therapist. Then she had the following healing dream. This first appeared in an interview I did with Sheila in 2015 for *DreamTime*, the IASD's magazine.

### Sheila's dream: The Dance of Healing

*There is a stage. It is dark. A small light shines on the upper left part of the stage. I am there now, in a beautiful, wispy, white ballet skirt. My massage therapist is beside me all in black except for his hands. His face is hidden. At first, I am still, like a wooden puppet. His hands slowly animate me, bringing me to life. Eventually the hood falls aside and his face is revealed. He takes me slowly through a series of ballet stretches—things I cannot possibly do on my own in waking life. With great tenderness he lifts me up into the air. My arms are outstretched and I feel as if I am flying. It is absolutely wonderful. I start to believe that it is possible, that I can indeed fly. Higher and higher . . .*

*My therapist lovingly places his hands and cheek on my belly. Through the dance, he has implanted his seed of healing within me and new life is stirring within. I am pregnant with my own healing. I am astonished. Now I am free to go off into the world and birth my own healing which will benefit others too. I am filled with awe and wonder.*

*I leave the stage, ready to return to my life.*

After this dream, the pain finally eased up for the first time in years. I finally felt strong enough to start exploring movement in my waking body. Having been plagued with chronic pain for so long, this was a great challenge. It meant viewing my body in a whole new way. Cultivating strength, flexibility, and grace rather than disassociating from the body to cope with pain. I decided it was time to try dancing in waking life.

It was incredibly terrifying! It took a tremendous amount of courage to step onto the dance floor for the first time. I was literally shaking throughout my body during those early lessons. Today, I dance at least two hours a day and take a private lesson weekly.

Now, I cannot imagine a day without dancing! Through dance, I have learned how to continue exploring and holding the dream in my body in the partnership with others, in a way that has deeply enhanced my art, teaching, and healing. I am eager to see where this new dance takes me.

---

The contrast in Sheila's dream is startling. She moves from the stuck energy of "I am still, like a wooden puppet" to burgeoning liberation as the dance frees her and she understands, "I can indeed fly [. . .] I am free to go off into the world and birth my own healing." This dream shows a remarkable transition, one that transformed the dreamer's life by radically altering her relationship with her own body.

Sheila's healing dream is a great example of how important bodywork is for those suffering from chronic pain and illness. We can learn to transform our relationship with our body. When we move our body, we release blocked energy and learn how to work in healing ways with the inner flow of energy we all have. People sometimes experience great resistance to bodywork, par-

ticularly if it feels difficult or painful to move, but when we combine gentle movement with energy work and our own healing
dream imagery, we stand a good chance of alleviating some of
our pain, so it is worth a try! If you are incapacitated through
pain or illness and cannot move your own body, you can still
benefit from bodywork in the form of shiatsu massage, acupres-
sure, and similar techniques where a natural health practitioner
can facilitate the flow of energy through your body. You can
actively participate in these sessions by focusing on your own
powerful healing dream imagery and imagining it penetrating
and transforming your pain or illness.

Choose a healing dream image you'd like to work with, and
try the practice below to bring healing energy into your body. If
you are too ill to rub your hands together, simply do the whole
exercise as a visualization, imagining yourself carrying out every
one of the actions and receiving the healing energy. Mental
imagery is a powerful tool for healing.

## PRACTICE #40

## THE HEALING ENERGY BALL

1. Stand tall with your feet slightly apart, arms relaxed at your
   sides, palms open. Close your eyes and experience for a
   moment the connection between sky and earth: your head in
   the sky, your feet on the earth. Breathe slowly in and out.
2. Eyes still closed, begin to rub your hands together as fast as you
   can, so that your palms grow warm. Feel the build-up of heat
   and friction.
3. Stop, and separate your palms ever so slightly, leaving only a
   few millimetres between them. Can you feel the space between
   your palms? It should be tingling and alive. If you can't feel
   anything, return to rubbing your hands together hard and fast.

4. Once you can feel the tingling heat between your palms, increase the distance between them, remaining focused on the space between them as it stretches wider.

5. Create a ball shape by loosely cupping your hands. This is your energy ball. Imagine that your energy ball has a color, or glows with light. Feel how flexible and elastic it is—it can grow or shrink effortlessly. Play with your energy ball by leaning your body to the left or to the right, or by increasing the distance between your hands. Raise the ball slowly into the air.

6. Imagine your healing dream image (see pages 86–87) appearing like a speck of light in the ball and growing into a clear, healing presence. If you don't have a specific healing dream image you want to work with, just visualize a healing golden light. The color or shape of your energy ball might change as the healing dream imagery fills it, and you can let this happen. Some people's energy balls will be as enormous as their outstretched arms can manage, while others' will be as small as an apple. As long as you can feel the ball, its size doesn't matter.

7. Balance your healing energy ball on top of your head and slowly bring your palms closer to your head until they are touching it. Let your ball dissolve into your body.

8. Without breaking contact with your body, bring your warm, energized hands to the areas of your body that need it—your hips, your knees, your belly, your eyes. Imagine healing energy flowing to where it's needed, easing pain and creating harmony.

9. Take a deep breath and open your eyes. Smile, knowing that you have done your body some good.

)———(

The following practice is a very relaxing one that can be lovely to do just as you go off to sleep at night. It's helpful for reconnecting with your most beautiful and healing dream imagery, and it's a nightly reminder to continue doing Mindful Dreamig so that you keep enjoying its benefits.

### PRACTICE #41

## FLOAT IN A HEALING POOL

1. Lie comfortably and close your eyes. Take deep, relaxing breaths and allow yourself to sink into a state close to sleep.

2. Visualize yourself floating in a pool of infinite, loving light. The light can be any color—perhaps your favorite color. Feel how amazing it is to be immersed in this healing pool of light.

3. Know that on the level of your deepest self, your soul, you are loved beyond belief.

4. Bring into this loving pool of light your most powerfully beautiful or healing dream images. These dream images reflect your best self. Allow them to increase your feeling of well-being.

5. Without breaking your deep relaxation, anchor this feeling of absolute well-being with a tiny gesture. You could lightly touch your thumb and forefinger together, or apply gentle pressure to your tongue with your teeth. This will make it easier for you to access this healing energy whenever you want to, by repeating the gesture.

6. You can either sink from this visualization straight into sleep, or wake up: take a deep breath, open your eyes, and smile.

# NINE

# Healing dreams for grief and loss

Technically speaking, we all face death from the moment we're conceived. The only certainty we have in life is that one day we will die. Yet in modern Western culture we shy away from this knowledge, and dying is often feared. Dreams can prepare the dying for death, prepare the dying person's loved ones for their death, and help bereaved people to come to terms with the loss of somebody they love.

Dreams give support and insight into the dying process. Dr. Monique Séguin is an expert in suicide prevention and bereavement and works as a hospice nurse at the West Island Palliative Care Residence in Canada. She has found that dreams can be used as therapeutic tools for the dying, as they bring the dreamer an awareness of where they are in the dying process. One of her patients, a ninety-year-old man, dreamed he was standing on a beach with two crows. One crow was trying to make him move forward, while the other was holding on to make him stay. The dream showed the man that while part of him was ready to die, the other part of him was still holding on to life. Although the patient always said, "I'm old, it's time for me to go," the dream mirrored his internal conflict and reflected his ambivalence about death. When end-of-life dreams are listened to and the dying person is encouraged to talk about them or do simple dreamplay, a real connection between the dying person and the caregiver or family member can be experienced and death can become easier to face.

End-of-life dreams and deathbed visions are very common, and it is important to listen to and support the dying person. When end-of-life dreams are shared with their families, these can unite them before death in healing ways. In a 2016 *New York Times* article, "A New Vision for Dreams of the Dying," the work of neurobiologist Dr. Christopher Kerr is discussed. Dr. Kerr believes that end-of-life dreams have a therapeutic function and can help not only the dying but also their families. One dying woman had nightmares in which she relived memories of being sexually abused when she was young. This horrified her family, but doctors were then able to give her antianxiety medication and she had a healing exchange with a priest before dying peacefully in her sleep. Dr. Kerr feels that listening to patients' dreams can help doctors to make the right choices about which medication to give to help them towards a good death, but he warns against sedating them too much: "Often when we sedate them, we are sterilizing them from their own dying process," he said. "They'll say, "You robbed me—I was with my wife." The dreams of the dying can help doctors to guide them towards "a good death."

In this chapter, we'll look at the dreams of those facing death and learn how to do dreamwork with a dying person. Then we'll move into the grief process and see how Mindful Dreaming can help with positive and negative bereavement dreams.

## Healing dreams for those facing death

Healing dreams for those imminently facing death may sound a paradox—after all, how can we heal when we're about to die? But in fact, people facing death are often readier than they have ever been in their lives to heal past rifts and face difficult truths. Dreams can help the dying to accept their own death. One woman had a series of lucid dreams leading up to her death in which she had profoundly spiritual experiences of floating bodiless in light. This helped her to accept that not only was death not "the end of everything" but that it was also a spiritual transition and not to be feared.

Dreams of the dying very often include transportation and deceased relatives such as parents or a spouse, who seem to be waiting for them and sometimes even urge them to join them. Dying patients often find solace in dreams of their own dead loved ones who have gone before them. Sometimes a dream house will represent the dying body. Artist Dr. Fariba Bogzaran, coauthor of *Integral Dreaming*, shared a lucid dream with me that she had when she was facing death. It appears in full in my fall 2014 "Amazing Dreamers" feature in *DreamTime*.

## Fariba's dream: On the Fringe of Death

*I am walking through a mansion that is falling apart. All the plaster is peeling off, the windows are shattered, the floor is uneven. There are many levels in this house. Through one level and staircase I see an opening into another world. It is beautiful and spacious. I am alone until I walk into a room. Four women are sitting in a chair in a circle facing each other. They are "fringing" a raw canvas.*

*The atmosphere is very quiet and contemplative. It feels like they are cloistered nuns. A voice says that this is a vehicle of meditation. In the center is a table with all the strings from the raw canvas. In the slowness of time, I become lucid. I want to remember the scene. I stand there witnessing the calmness of their presence in light of the destruction of the mansion.*

I had this dream when I was battling a potentially fatal health situation. I had lost twenty pounds with no end in sight and was facing many unpleasant symptoms. I was preparing myself for the inevitable. While seeking medical and alternative help, I was also closing chapters in my life and was preparing to leave. I would spend hours being with nature, floating in the sea, breathing in as much of life as possible. I had bought several raw canvases to do painting. I was preparing them by fringing the top and bottom. Because I had so little energy, all I could do was fringe both sides of the canvases and leave them blank.

The dream was obviously the reflection of my dying body. The counsel of the elder women in my dream, who had appeared in other dreams, was teaching me a method of dying or healing. Was I going to die or heal? I prepared for both.

After the dream above, I began fringing the canvas as a mode of meditation. I would pay great attention to each thread and think of how my life was "hanging on a thread!" At one point, the action began taking me inside a particular zone. I felt the action was total mindfulness. I attribute the wise elders' method as one of the vehicles for my healing.

---

In the midst of a life-threatening illness, Fariba's lucid dream gave her a practical task to enable her to become meditative and mindful in order to allow healing to take place. She followed the dream's advice, and she did not die. Instead, she healed and simultaneously created a new art form, decorating her home with blank, fringed canvases.

### Distressing end-of-life dreams

Dreams of the dying occasionally come too late to help the dreamer. One man in palliative care who didn't have a good relationship with his children dreamed he had a diamond in his hand. He wanted to give it to someone but no one wanted it. After this dream, he became very agitated. He died that same night.

Given the context, I think this is one of the saddest dreams I've heard. Imagine feeling such agitation and rejection at the end of a long life! What a waste. Our time on this planet is so short; we are like fireworks lighting the sky for a few bright seconds. What we do with our time, how we live our lives, the relationships we have, how we help others: these are the important things. Too late, this man discovered he had a precious gift to share but nobody was interested in it. What an unfortunate way to leave this life, with a sense of unfinished business and regret. He might have been able to reach a greater level of peace before his death if he had worked just briefly with his dream, simply imagining a scene where his children (or someone—anyone!) stepped forward to receive his diamond.

PRACTICE #42:

## HOW TO DO DREAMWORK WITH A DYING PERSON

1. Listen attentively. Listening is an incredibly supportive therapeutic act in its own right.
2. Don't judge or leap to interpret the dream. The dream belongs to the dreamer. It might simply be enough for them to share their dream, without any further dreamwork. You can help them to unwrap the meaning of their dream if they want you to, by sharing any of the techniques in chapter 2 for understanding dreams.
3. If the dream is obviously upsetting for the dying person, ask them, "If you could change the story of your dream for the better, what would happen?" If they seem stumped, remind them that, for example, they can get help in the dream; send love to the people in the dream and see them transform; support their dreaming self by offering advice or comfort; or change the ending of the dream so that they have a good feeling about it.
4. If the new dream story they choose feels forced or hollow to them, they haven't found the right one yet. Only when the new

scenario fully resonates with them have they hit on the right story for them.

5. Once they find a scenario that makes them feel good, suggest that they vividly imagine this happier scenario taking place, really feeling it on an emotional level. They can repeat this step as often as they like, to create a happier inner movie.

6. Being heard by you, and doing these few steps of dreamwork, is very likely to lift the spirits of the dying person considerably. Doing dreamwork with someone can be a strong bonding experience and they will feel your empathy and support throughout.

)———(

People faced with their own mortality can change enormously in a short space of time. Whenever healing takes place, even if it is just hours or minutes before death, it is worthwhile as it can help the dying to go into death more peacefully and provide the family with solace. Dreams of the dying sometimes provide the dreamer with a glimpse of paradise; a vision of what it may be like after we transition from our physical body and enter the after-death state. "This is vast. You would not believe how vast it is," one man told his wife. When my grandmother was on her deathbed, she said, "Dying is beautiful." Granny gave me one last piece of advice before she died: "Make the best of it."

Perhaps this is something we all owe to those we love who have died before us: to make the best of this precious life of ours.

### There may be life after death

Research into near-death experiences (NDEs) has increased and become more scientific in recent years. In an NDE, people who nearly die often report experiences such as traveling down a tunnel, moving towards a bright light, seeing deceased relatives, and experiencing feelings of total love, bliss, and peace before they are "sent back" to their physical body. In 2014, the results of the world's largest study of NDEs were released. The AWARE study (AWAreness during REsuscitation) involved 2,060 patients and was led by Dr. Sam Parnia. It investigated the NDE accounts of people who had been declared clinically dead and were then resuscitated. The results showed that death doesn't take place at one moment and is potentially reversible. A linked area of NDE research explores deathbed visions and dreams of the dying.

There is a great fear of death in our culture. Yet death is a natural transition. Accounts of NDEs suggest that dying may be a joyful release; a return to oneness. It is good to respect the dreams of the dying as they can be influential in illuminating this final journey.

All of us, not just the dying, can confront our fear of death and dying in dreams. One lucid dreamer I know was confronted by a spooky figure like something from a horror film. She was told by the dream that this figure was her fear of death. Lucid, she was able to transform her fear into acceptance, and the moment she did, she was lifted into a luminous light. When she awoke, she knew she had conquered her fear of death.

Even if we feel OK with the idea of death and dying, for many of us it is not the fear of our own death that is problematic, but the grief we know we will feel when those we love die. Let's have a look at the grief process and how Mindful Dreaming can help.

## Mindful Dreaming and the grief process

We can get stuck in our grief. Dreams help us to move on from this stuck position and heal. Dreaming of a deceased loved one allows us to maintain a connection with them that can ease the grieving process. Instead of drowning in loss, we can begin to understand death as a natural part of life and trust that our loved one is OK. Dreams can provide a beautiful, healing link between the dead and those who miss them.

Everybody grieves differently depending on the severity of their loss, their personality type, and their philosophy of life, which includes their religion and their beliefs about what happens after death. Grief does not have an expiration date. It is an ongoing process and takes as long as it takes. Mindful Dreaming can ease this process by bringing comfort in the form of healing dreamplay and by helping to maintain a sense of connection with the deceased.

There are two main types of grief dreams: positive and negative. In positive bereavement dreams, the deceased person is usually present in the dream, often looking young and happy or glowing with light. There is the strong sense that they are OK. The deceased person may give advice or reassurance that everything will be fine for the dreamer. Words of comfort are spoken; forgiveness is exchanged, or a hug. Sometimes the deceased person is present only as an emotion or a sensation of light or warmth. In positive bereavement dreams there is no need for further dreamwork. The healing imagery and the sense of comfort it brings can be meditated on whenever it feels right.

Keep a dream journal and allow your dreams to show you where you are emotionally as you go through the grief process. Use techniques such as "Take a healing breath" (see page 87) to integrate highly positive dream imagery as you go about your life.

## Positive bereavement dreams

Even the darkest nights of the soul are lit up by dreams. Bereavement, loss, abandonment, and fear of death can be eased by dreams of tremendous solace. Dr. Laurel Clark, President Emeritus of the School of Metaphysics in Missouri, had this dream on the evening of September 11, 2001, after hearing about the attacks on the Twin Towers. Her husband, John, had passed away a year before:

> *John is in New York, helping the people who have died in the World Trade Center. He looks beautiful, radiant, and healthy. I ask him with alarm, "Are they OK?" When I say that, he beams a brilliant smile and his whole being lights up with an effulgence I have never before experienced.*
>
> *"Yes," he says emphatically, "They're fine. Once they're out they're fine!" I feel a whoosh of exhilaration. I know he means that once the people who have died are out of the body, they are fine. Their spirits are free!*

This dream changed Laurel's life in numerous ways. It was personally healing because she got to see her husband looking healthy and radiant. Laurel also found the dream healing in a global sense. As a minister and counselor, people sought her counsel in the aftermath of 9/11. Today, Laurel shares her dream to help people who are grieving the loss of a loved one or facing their own impending death. She feels that the message, "Once we are out of the body, we're fine!" seems universal. Laurel says this dream changed her from being a believer to a knower that life exists eternally.

Lucid dreamers can ask to see a deceased loved one as soon as they wake up inside a dream, and all dreamers can incubate a healing dream of the deceased to help them through the grief process. There is much comfort and joy to be found in such encounters. When we work with healing dreams in the bereavement process, we begin to view our dead loved ones as continuing sources of love, solace, and wisdom. Clinical psychologist Dr. Patricia Garfield shared a bereavement dream with me that appears in full in my "Amazing Dreamers" feature in the Spring 2014 edition of *DreamTime*. This powerful healing dream arose when Patricia was still struggling to cope with grief three years after the loss of her beloved husband Zal after thirty-three years of marriage.

---

## Patricia's dream: The Great Baptism

*A wise woman speaks of a coin (the coin of life?). I see it, large, with a deckled edge. The gist of her talk is that the two sides are indivisibly linked, the love and the pain, but somehow it's all OK: life is whole. The highlight of all this talk is to be my baptism/initiation by this wise woman into the group.*

*I get ready to undergo the special ceremony. Naked, I step into a white porcelain bathtub filled with water. The tub is encircled by loving people. As I lie in the bubbling water, the woman says, "Make ready for . . ." At this, she tosses into the water a purple powder. The entire tub buzzes and fizzes with the effect of the powder. I feel a tingling all over my body. Every part of me is tingling; the purple powdered bubbles are roiling the water and penetrating deep into my bones. I sense loving people around me and Zal caring for me as I undergo this—what?— transformation? The feeling is very powerful. As my eyes close in the dream, anticipating submersion, I open them in life.*

I had been in grief therapy since Zal's death, trying to figure out how to move my life forward while I continued to feel raw and ripped in half. Coins in my dreams often indicate "change" in my waking life. This coin was huge, suggesting a gigantic change. The Great Baptism dream had a profound effect on my state of being in the world. I felt a greater acceptance of the fact of my husband's loss. The dream marked a shift in my grieving process from despair and suffering to a more active attempt to find a new way of living without the physical presence of my loved and loving man. This was, indeed, a "big change."

I sensed that something of each spirit continues beyond death. I felt more hopeful. I was forced to confront the fact that great love and great loss are indivisibly linked, that suffering from loss of a great love is in fact the measure of its value. Would I have wanted to not have experienced such love? No. Then I must accept the cost of its loss. Immersed in the tub of "bone-deep change," I no longer felt alone in this task.

---

## PRACTICE #43

### INCUBATE A DREAM
### OF A DECEASED LOVED ONE

I have had people come up to me with tears in their eyes and ask what they can do in order to have a dream of their deceased loved one. When we long to see and touch our loved one again in a dream, and hanker for the feeling—however fleeting—that they are with us, their absence from our dreams can be wrenching. Here are some tips for incubating a dream:

1. Practice this simple relaxation technique for a minute or two whenever you can during the day, to calm your emotions. (When people see deceased loved ones in a dream, sometimes they are so overwhelmed with emotion that they wake instantly, which they then feel very disappointed about.) Sit down, close your eyes, and breathe slowly in and out. On the in-breath, inhale peace and calmness. On the out-breath, release pain, sadness, or any strong emotions. Breathe right out to the very end of your breath, as this encourages a deeper, fresher in-breath. Doing this breathing exercise as you walk outside in the fresh air will help you even more as it will ground you by connecting you with nature and the earth.

2. As you fall asleep, summon a mental picture of your loved one and think to yourself, "Tonight I will see you in my dreams." Smile at the thought of seeing them again, and as you lie in the darkness, imagine how the dream might play out. If you find

yourself getting upset, stop this process. Try to feel a gentle sense of anticipation as you imagine the dream meeting, and then go calmly off to sleep.

3. Sometimes the force of our grief may paradoxically be what stops us from dreaming about the deceased. Grief is exhausting. When we are exhausted, the body needs deep, recuperative sleep and it may be harder to recall dreams. If this is the case for you, return to the "Sleep well; dream well" section on page 17, and focus on regaining your strength before incubating a dream of your loved one.

4. When you wake up in the night (we all do; many times, but usually only for a couple of seconds as we change position), recall your desire to see your loved one in a dream. Again, hold this intention only lightly, without allowing yourself to get swept off on a wave of strong emotion.

5. Keep a dream journal every day as this will bring you into closer contact with your dreams and you'll be far less likely to miss a dream of your deceased loved one. They may first appear in unobtrusive ways: you might fleetingly see their face among a large group of people, or you may just know that they are behind you in a dream, without actually seeing them. In time, such glimpses or sensations may expand into an actual dream meeting. If you don't dream directly of your deceased loved one, any dreams with healing elements such as beautiful nature or healthy animals can be used as healing imagery to meditate on and help you in the grief process as you find a new way of being in the world.

)———(

## Understanding negative bereavement dreams

Many bereavement dreams provide us with comfort and a more accepting sense of closure. The fact of seeing the deceased person in vibrant health in a dream and somehow knowing that they are all right can be incredibly healing. But some bereavement dreams are anything but comforting and need to be worked on to relieve the distressing emotions. The circumstances of death can make a big difference to how the bereaved person reacts. If a loved one has committed suicide or died in a horrific accident, this traumatic bereavement is likely to bring a greater number of troubled dreams than those that might follow the peaceful death of a ninety-four-year-old grandfather.

In negative bereavement dreams, the situation is not a happy one. There may be feelings of anger, bitterness, betrayal, resentment, fear, or a heart-breaking sense of unfinished business. The dreamer may argue with the deceased loved one in the dream. The dead person may berate the dreamer, or even chase them. Since dreams are often symbolic, the deceased person may not appear but might be represented instead by unhealthy imagery or upsetting events. Dreams are emotional mirrors, showing us how we really feel. Negative bereavement dreams highlight the psychological complexity of the dreamer's relationship with the deceased, or the dreamer's inability to accept their loss. These dreams can be worked with for greater understanding and to release overly negative powerful emotions.

If your dreams are disturbing, Lucid Dreamplay techniques such as the "How to transform nightmares" practice on page 125, or Lucid Writing, can be useful in enabling your inner dream movie to change into something that feels more healing and accepting, to help you release difficult emotions and move forward into a new stage in the grief process.

Artist and dreamworker Victoria's dream occurred eight months after the death of her elderly mother, with whom she had a difficult relationship. It contained toxic dream imagery that Victoria worked with in a Lucid Writing session with me. As this example shows, it is often helpful to use more than one dreamwork technique on a dream. Use your intuition—if you don't feel you have really "cracked" the dream, try a different practice.

---

### Victoria's dream: Black Widow Spiders

*I've been cleaning and clearing Mother's vast bedroom. Black widow spiders are hanging from the ceiling. I've been able to swat the cobwebs away with a broom in the past, but these hanging spider lines are more tenacious. My tiny, fragile, old mother shuffles towards the bed. I see that there is still more cleaning work to be done. The black widow spiders are now under the bed, out of sight. I know what to do. I will do the final cleaning and clearing with the power of a vacuum.*

Writing with the voice of an element in the dream can reveal insight into what exactly this dream image means to you, the dreamer. Victoria could have chosen any element from her dream: her mother, the bed, or even the ceiling. She decided to write with the voice of the spider.

### Lucid Writing from the perspective of the spider

*I am the Black Widow. I have a venomous bite. I inflict a fatal poison if I perceive a threat to my life force. I am a sexual cannibal. I eat my men after mating. I am patient; I can lie in wait for my victims. I have suspended myself from a dragline that is strong and unbreakable.*

Then Victoria simply focused on her dream and allowed her thoughts, associative memories, and emotions to spill out onto the page unchecked.

### Lucid Writing about the bed

*No one else may touch Mother's bed but me. I must cleanse myself before touching her bed linens. I must make the bed her way . . .*

*against my own casual nature . . . Something is always wrong and not right. Corrections must be made. Our weekly time together, making her big bed. A time of sharing: her sharing, not mine. All about Mother, never about me. No regard for me. No one else may listen to Mother's sad life but me.*

## Victoria's insights into her dream

Although my mother is the main character in my dream, I came to understand that each of the other images within the dream symbolize different aspects of her. The spider, and more surprisingly the bed, revealed the deeper complexity of our relationship. I have denied many of my emotions over the years of indentured servitude to my mother's dominance. The black widow spider is a reflection of Mother's toxicity. The bed image explores her insistence on my complete compliance.

Working with the dream symbols through Lucid Writing has a power that cuts right to the bone of my core issues with my mother. Lucid Writing now helps me find the tools for the task of cleaning and clearing our relationship as I move through and beyond her cannibalistic relationship with me.

---

Victoria's Lucid Writing shows how it is possible to begin to move beyond a toxic or unhealthy relationship we had with someone who is deceased. Black widow spiders wrap their prey in silk (like bed covers). They have fangs. They inject poison that liquefies the corpse of their prey. This is an extremely powerful, toxic dream image. The resourceful dreamer, an experienced dreamworker, already thinks of the solution of the vacuum cleaner in the dream, to finish up the work of clearing this toxicity away. The dream flags up the fact that work still needs to be done in order to free the dreamer from the toxic remains of her relationship with her mother, while showing her that she has the right tool to do this work. Even when a person is dead, we can still heal our relationship with them by listening to our dreams and doing Lucid Dreamplay.

## Working with distressing dreams of deceased loved ones

One woman shared this dream with me: *I am in a room with my mother, who died four months ago. She is upset, screaming at me. I feel terrible, and wake up believing that she is unhappy in death.* Using the "Dream Talk technique" (see page 38), she re-entered this dream while awake and was able to talk to her mother. In response to her question, "Mother, why are you so upset with me?" the mother answered, "It's not you I'm upset with!" As the conversation progressed, the woman realized that her mother had always found situations to be unhappy about while she was alive, and was simply acting "in character" in the dream.

This dream did not mean that her mother was suffering in death; it was just showing the dreamer an aspect of her relationship with her mother, as she had so often felt targeted by her mother's negativity and drama. Armed with this insight, the dreamer was able to hug her mother in the dream replay and feel a flash of peaceful forgiveness. This was the first step in working in a healing way with her bereavement dreams to help her through the grieving process.

As you know, the point of Lucid Dreamplay is *not* to whitewash unpleasant dream images and emotions into fake positive ones. The point is to gain insight into life, relationships, ourselves, and others. For this reason, dreamplay should never be forced. If you feel as though you are forcing a disturbing dream image to turn into something more wholesome, or forcing a dream person to respond in a certain way, it's best to drop the exercise and try again when you are feeling more relaxed and open. Spontaneous change that is experienced on an emotional level is a sure sign that the dreamplay is working to bring you healing imagery. Give this version of the Dream Talk technique a try, as it can be powerfully beneficial and you'll soon get the hang of it!

## PRACTICE #44:

# DREAM TALK FOR BEREAVEMENT DREAMS

1. Relax. Re-enter your dream by closing your eyes, breathing calmly, and reliving the imagery, environment, sensations, and emotions. Know that you can stop the process at any time if it becomes too difficult by taking a deep breath and opening your eyes.

2. Focus on the dream figure you want to talk to. See them and feel their energy and mood. Calmly ask them why they said what they just said, or why they seem agitated. Be prepared for anything: the dream figure may react defensively, begin to cry, or refuse to answer at first.

3. Patiently continue to attempt to communicate with them in your imagination. Observe them carefully, noticing any changes in their expression or body language. Don't put words into their mouth; instead, leave pauses for them to respond. This way you are much more likely to get a meaningful response.

4. If at any time you feel distressed, imagine protective white light all around you, keeping you safe and calm. Offer the dream figure reassurance and understanding. Send them love and healing light.

5. If you are talking to a deceased loved one, say any words of love or forgiveness that you didn't get to say to them before they died. It can be enormously therapeutic to say words of love or share your deepest feelings, even in your imagination.

Doing this releases emotions that we have bottled up inside us, and allows us to really feel the love or forgiveness. Imagine the person receiving your words and responding to them. If you become distressed, mentally bathe yourself and the other person in love and light. You can always return to this process another day.

6. When you are ready, return to normal waking consciousness by taking a deep breath and opening your eyes. If you feel emotional, be sure to eat and drink and generally take care of your body. Write down or draw any healing moments and cherish them, returning to them for solace whenever you need to.

)————(

PRACTICE #45:

# LIVE YOUR BEST LIFE—STARTING NOW!

Change your life now, while you can. When we listen to the dreams of the dying, major themes come through: unfinished business; the need to forgive or to be forgiven; love lost or withheld; regret that we did not have a closer relationship with our children or parents. Why wait a lifetime before realizing too late that we did not lead the life we would have loved to lead? In palliative nurse Bronnie Ware's 2009 blog article "Regrets of the Dying," which led to her bestselling book on the subject, she notes the five biggest regrets people have on their deathbed:

1. I wish I'd had the courage to live a life true to myself, not the life others expected of me.
2. I wish I hadn't worked so hard.
3. I wish I'd had the courage to express my feelings.

4. I wish I had stayed in touch with my friends.
5. I wish that I had let myself be happier.

Try this short exercise: imagine yourself at the end of your life, looking back on the way you have lived it. Write five sentences, each beginning with the words "I wish . . ." Try to express your deepest regrets. Once you have your five "deathbed regrets," write a further five sentences to rectify these, each beginning "I will . . ." For example, if one regret is, "I wish I had been there more for my brother when he needed me most," you might then write, "I will always follow my intuition and be there when I know people need me most."

Look at your second list often and begin the work needed to change what needs to be changed. Happiness is a choice. When we are alert to our own ability to transform our lives, and when we allow our dreams to guide us through the ups and downs of life, we can create a better life—and a better death!—for ourselves and others.

Dreams can guide us to our best life, our happiest life; a life filled with love and meaning . . . and, finally, into a peaceful death.

# TEN

# Soul dreams
## *dream your way to happiness*

Soul dreams are luminous dreams that have a special intensity or power for us: they are dreams of the higher; of spirit and soul—and they feel deeply significant. They strike us with their vivid beauty or profound mystery and are not easily forgotten. These dreams seem to emerge fully formed from the dreamer's soul. Carl Jung called such life-changing dreams "the richest jewel[s] in the treasure-house of psychic experience" and emphasized their psychological and spiritual importance. Soul dreams can help us to unlock our deepest potential and discover our life's purpose.

A man in one of my workshops related what was clearly a soul dream: he was walking up a lit stairway to heaven. As he walked up, his clothes were falling off him. Such a dream may reflect the dreamer's advancement on his spiritual journey; moving towards the light and revealing the naked self. Soul dreams are not necessarily rooted in formal religion by any means, but may sometimes include aspects of the dreamer's personal religious beliefs or upbringing. Many soul dreams simply resonate with us spiritually without including religious concepts or icons. When I was twenty, I dreamed that a beautiful large orb of orange light-energy materialized in front of my wardrobe. Lucidly aware, I watched in awe as it floated there. It had a powerful, loving, female energy. Without words, it told me it would always be there whenever I needed it. Soul dreams connect us with the deep source of light and knowledge that we all have somewhere within us.

### The main characteristics of soul dreams

◊ Light: this might be a glowing sunset, luminously beautiful people or animals, bright colors, or an all-encompassing experience of imageless light

◊ A spiritual quality: a sense of divine presence, mystery, or deep significance

◊ Exceptionally vibrant nature; people and animals that exude health and liveliness

◊ Powerful emotions such as joy, nostalgia, unconditional love, desire, sorrow, or a profound sense of safety or belonging

◊ Archetypal or symbolic imagery

◊ Music that profoundly moves the dreamer

◊ The presence of wisdom and compassion—these may come in the form of a dream person, or the dreamer may simply "know" something in the dream

Although not all of these characteristics will be present in a soul dream, one element that nearly all soul dreams appear to share is luminosity, or light. There are two types of soul dream:

1. Soul dreams where there is no imagery—nothing but light
2. Cinematic soul dreams with vivid imagery

Both types of soul dream involve light. In this chapter, first of all we'll look at the value and significance of light in dreams and explore lucid dreams where all imagery vanishes and there is nothing but light. Then we'll move on to examine examples of soul dreams that have a flow of imagery. We'll see how all soul dreams can increase our happiness.

## Light in dreams

Light in dreams tends to signify a connection to spirit and soul, which is why light is characteristic of soul dreams. Light in dreams is also linked to healing: the reports of many lucid dreamers show that being bathed in light in a dream, or seeing the dream scene glow as if lit from within, is associated with psychological or even physical healing.

Look for the light in your dreams! In any dream, move towards the light. This might be luminescent imagery or an overall glowing. Russian dream researcher Dr. Maria Volchenko showed me an oil painting she had done of her recurring dream. It was a nighttime scene of a glowing green tree with a tigress at the base of the trunk. Sitting low in the tree branches, reaching out a hand to the tigress, was a person made entirely of light. At first glance, I saw that this was a soul dream: luminous imagery, strong emotion, the figure of light, the powerful dream animal, beautiful nature.

In your dream journal, note down any experiences of light or luminous dream imagery. Notice which dream images are particularly luminous, and ask yourself what this imagery means to you, using free-association or any of the other techniques in chapter 2. Dreams with luminous imagery are often soul dreams.

Up until this point, we have looked at dreams as inner movies and explored how we can change this inner movie in healing ways to help us with illness, grief, or in supporting our younger selves. Now we're going to take a step further, and look at soul dreams where the inner movie ceases and we experience nothing but light.

## Dreams where there is nothing but light

In lucid dreams, we can go beyond the splendid inner movie imagery typical of dreaming and seek out experiences of meditation, peace, and enlightenment. The deeper reality of the dream is glimpsed and these glimpses help us to become more lucid in waking life. I've had many dream experiences of floating in what I call the Lucid Light. Often, this is a dream space with nothing in it—no objects, people, or animals; no buildings or dreamscapes; no sounds. It's a quite wonderful emptiness made entirely of light. It can look like bright white clouds, or sparkling blackness. It can be grey dots, or luminous orange. Lucid in a dream, you can float in this light and experience an incredible feeling of oneness, as if you've returned to the source of all life and belong in this peaceful, healing space. There is often no sense of having a dream body any more, just a sense of soaring completeness and safety. It is like being bathed in pure love.

Countless similar experiences from advanced lucid dreamers all over the world and throughout history point to the fact that this space of formless light is not dependent on cultural beliefs, but transcends religious and cultural boundaries. We may all experience it every night, as a sort of gap between dreams or a deep sleep state. But we tend to forget it, because it's hard to recall something so formless. I believe the Lucid Light is the baseline state of consciousness from which all of our conscious experience emerges. The Lucid Light can be any color—white, grey, purple, emerald green, orange, or even black.

Sometimes in dreams I fly at great speed through white light—which I call "soul-flying," as it feels so spiritual to be bodiless, conscious, and free. Other times, I float in colored light. One lady I worked with did a floating meditation in a light-filled lucid dream and experienced first happiness and then ecstasy. She reports, "When I woke up, I felt such well-being, such lightness!" These light-filled soul dreams leave the dreamer with a residue of bliss and oneness that carries over into waking life, coloring interactions, healing relationships, and creating harmonious connections.

People who have these experiences of floating in light often find that their perspective on life changes. Following profound experiences in the Lucid Light, they lose their fear of death because they understand on a deep level that death is not the end of everything, but a natural transition from one state to another. For thousands of years, Tibetan Buddhists have claimed that lucid dreaming can be a way of practicing conscious dying, especially when the dream imagery vanishes and we have a pure experience of the light. The Tibetans believe that practicing mindfulness and dream lucidity enables us to wake up at the moment of death and transcend the cycle of rebirth so that we attain spiritual bliss.

If training yourself to wake up at the moment of death sounds a little ambitious to you for now, simply imagine you are in a holistic wellness center, inside a flotation tank. You are entirely relaxed. You can't feel where the water starts and ends around your body, or which way up you are, or how long you've been inside the tank. This timeless, blissful experience can be enjoyed without even leaving your bed. When we get used to floating bodiless (and painless) in what feels like infinite dream space, it can be deeply healing: think of it as a free flotation tank experience! Lucid Light soul dreams can give us the ultimate wellness experience. We can have experiences of peace and harmony so deep and satisfying that we wake up from them feeling happier.

## PRACTICE #46

## HOW TO NAVIGATE LUCID LIGHT SOUL DREAMS

If you find yourself lucidly experiencing a dream that has no objects in it, no furniture, no buildings or rooms, only an expanse of colored light or black light; don't panic or be afraid. Think of it as a fantastic opportunity to explore pure conscious awareness . . . and have a relaxing spa experience at the same time!

1. If you want to experience a Lucid Light soul dream, as soon as you become lucid, try leaving the dream you're in. You can do this by diving through a door or window, or into a pool, or flying up into the sky as far as you can go.

2. You can be intrepid and try shooting along at great speed, or build a dream by projecting your thoughts, intentions, and visualizations onto the empty dream canvas. Or you can decide to kick back and enjoy being bodiless and pain-free for once.

3. Meditating in this state is incredibly easy because there are no distractions—no body; nothing much to look at or listen to. It's just you and the vastness of dream space. You have become a dreaming version of an astronaut.

4. Surrendering to the Lucid Light can provoke feelings of safety, oneness, bliss, and a sense of being loved unconditionally. These feelings rejuvenate us and we wake up feeling profoundly refreshed, as if we've been on the best spa weekend ever. Experiencing the serenity of light-filled dreams can restore us to a state of health and well-being.

One lucid dreamer had recurring nightmares about tornadoes until he overcame his fear and decided in the dream to see what the storm was like from within. Instantly an invisible force lifted him into the tornado. Inside the storm were translucent whiteness and a tremendous feeling of peace. When we connect with the inner light we all have within us, we experience healing: our self-understanding grows, as does our awareness of the purpose of our life.

Now that we've seen how light can be a healing and spiritual element in dreams, let's explore soul dreams that involve a stream of dream imagery, usually with luminous colors, beauty, or the appearance of light in some other form.

## Soul dreams with imagery

Soul dreams generally appear as a visual inner movie, just as most dreams do. They differ from other types of dreams because they tend to be luminous and memorable and often focus on our life as a whole, rather than illuminating just one aspect of it. Soul dreams can accompany us for a lifetime, as they speak to us on a spiritual level. They invite our attention because when we unwrap them, they often reveal insights into our life path. Those that seem to present us with choices can become riddles that take years to understand, as with the following dream from Iain, dream scholar and emeritus reader in anthropology. Iain resolved this forty-year-old dream in a workshop with me, through Lucid Writing.

---

### Iain's dream: Indian Prince and Teapot Choice

*A beautiful Indian prince wearing purple and with some kind of headdress offers me a choice between a square and a round teapot.*

I had this dream in 1975 while living in Soho, London, working as a social work student in a homeless shelter. I had recently been on a fast, more or less for three days: the only time that I have done this! The imagery and the choice felt very powerful. I have always felt the dream represented a key choice about my persona, even my spiritual path. I felt the round teapot represented my religious upbringing as a Christian while the square one represented another, less usual, pathway.

I have worked with this imagery and those issues in different dreamwork settings over the past forty years. In the workshop, I finally resolved this dream.

### Iain's Lucid Writing as the Indian prince

*I am a part of you; emissary of the Divine in you; I gave you a koan to work on for forty years; now you don't need it any more . . . you answered the riddle. Now for the integration of both religions and all. I gave you this puzzle and you have loved it.*

## Iain's reflections

The message I received by becoming the Indian prince, my unconscious figure, was that I'd had a forty-year koan (in Zen Buddhism, an impossible task set by a Zen master) to work with and I had come to realize that I didn't need to choose between two Abrahamic religions but that I was enabled, via my interest and work with dreams, to relate to the idea of the Abrahamic religions as a whole since the God/Godhead of all three was exactly the same.

This felt like the breakthrough of a predicament.

———————————————————————————

Iain's dream shows the extraordinary ability of the dreaming mind to summarize a life-long spiritual dilemma in a short dream, using an everyday object like a teapot. Yet this is clearly a soul dream, as shown by the beautiful Indian prince with his purple clothes and headdress. It takes the dreamer forty years to understand that he didn't need to choose between the round and square teapots (or between Christianity and Islam), but this delayed understanding is not a bad thing. Indeed, the dream provoked him into thinking deeply about his spiritual path over the course of more than half a lifetime, and during that time Iain has done important scholarly work into the role of dreams in Christianity and Islam. The resolution of his dream doubtless arrived at the perfect time.

Soul dreams can be mysterious, provocative gifts that can be unwrapped time and again, revealing powerful new insights as the dreamer moves from one phase of life into the next.

PRACTICE #47

## THE SIX-STEP PROGRAM
## TO HAVING SOUL DREAMS

The wonderful thing about lucid dreaming is that you can guide the dream into a soulful, spiritual experience as soon as you realize that you are dreaming. I've created a six-step program below to help you do this. First, here's a quick reminder of what to focus on if you would like to have more lucid dreams. When you are mindful in waking life, you become more mindful in sleep, too, so work on being present to everything in your life: notice this moment, right now, with all your attention and senses. Communicate with your dreams by remembering them and writing them down. Meditate when you can. Practice recognizing different sleep states and their bodily sensations by watching the presleep imagery that appears in the darkness behind your closed eyes. Pay attention to your body so that you'll notice the difference when you are in your dream body. Take afternoon naps so you go straight into dream-rich REM sleep.

1. **Get good at having lucid dreams.** Use all the tips above and in chapter 3 to help you to have regular lucid dreams. The more experienced you are at lucid dreaming, the more likely you are to be able to guide your dream into becoming a soul dream.
2. **Practice feeling safe.** The biggest obstacle to having a spiritual experience in a dream is fear. Practice calm breathing during the day and practice creating an egg of protective light around your body. Use this—and your logical knowledge that you will wake safely from this dream—whenever you feel frightened in a dream. When you are fearless, curious, and open, you are ready to do deep lucid dreaming and bring back to your waking life feelings of oneness, peace, and joyfulness.

3. **Dive into the void.** As soon as you become lucid in a dream, stabilize the dream by staying calm, touching objects to ground you in the dream, or rubbing your hands together and repeating, "I am lucid." Then you could either dive through the dream into the lucid void, or just close your eyes and allow the dream to dissolve around you, while keeping your focus on having a soul dream.

4. **Meditate.** Meditation in a lucid dream is an incredibly fast way of reaching a spiritual experience, and meditation is *much* easier in a dream as we have no physical body to distract us! You might want to sit down cross-legged in the dream to meditate, but this isn't necessary: simply deciding to meditate and then closing your eyes can be enough.

5. **Pray or sing.** Praying or singing religious songs can also be a great way of focusing on a higher spiritual power and can lead to transcendent experiences.

6. **Ask the dream for help.** Anything can happen, and your only job is to stay lucid and not wake up, which can feel like a fine balance at first. Be open and see how the dream responds. You could simply ask the dream for help—"I'd like to float bodiless in healing light"—or (for the brave ones among you), "Show me the ultimate nature of reality!" or "Show me my soul."

⟩————⟨

Many soul dreams arise spontaneously at times in our lives when we need clarification, support, or succor. The following soul dream is one of my own that I had in 2016 while working simultaneously on three different dream books.

### Clare's dream: There Are Gifts Everywhere

*I'm in a chill-out lounge bar with a magnificent ocean view. A waiter holding a basket piled high with slices of bread offers me one. I decline because I've already eaten five slices, and there will be a big dinner later. But the waiter is politely insistent. He takes one of the slices of bread and lays it on my belly. I look up at him in surprise and notice that he is extraordinarily beautiful, with clear eyes. I explain why I don't need the bread, and hand it back to him. He smiles, but when he moves on, I notice he has placed the bread back on my belly!*

*Then I'm walking in some beautiful, vibrant woods, and I notice I'm holding two glasses of wine, one in each hand. This is far too much: I'm at an IASD dream conference and I want to keep a clear head. I look to my right and see a carpet of daffodils meandering through the forest. Other women from the conference are picking large bouquets of these daffodils. I'm happy not to pick any because as soon as you pick a flower, it begins to die.*

*Again, I look to my right. I see an amazing branch on the forest floor. Its green leaves curl in spectacular fashion. It has fallen from the tree like a ripe fruit and is there for the taking. I pick it up and think, "This is perfect; I'll accept this gift from the forest." I feel overwhelmed with gratitude and joy.*

The luminous colors, the natural beauty, and the profound joy at the end, mark this as a soul dream. This dream offers nourishment for the body (bread), the spirit (wine), and the soul (daffodils and the branch). Bread and wine are also sacraments in the Christian religion, symbolizing a bridge to the spiritual world. When I worked on the dream using the "Share a dream with a friend" technique (see page 81), at the end of the second telling I used the words, "I've finally found my gift!" As soon as I'd said that, my body started tingling from the waist all down my legs: a sure sign for me of an Aha moment.

The dream is about finding my gift. The dream kept offering me gifts that I felt I already had enough of, or didn't want more of. The dream seemed to be telling me to go with my intuition and I would find "the right gift" eventually (notice the way I repeatedly looked to the right in my dream). I seemed to have more than enough body-food and spirit-food, but what I was truly happy to accept was soul-food.

When I did Lucid Writing on this dream, four statements jumped out at me when I read back through what I'd written: 1) There are gifts everywhere. 2) The universe wants to give—all we have to do is say YES! 3) I've finally found my gift. 4) I'm about to birth three books.

"I've finally found my gift" felt like a statement about where I am in my life; a confirmation that I'm on the right path, writing my dream books, helping people with Mindful Dreaming, and exploring lucid dreaming to discover more about the nature of reality, consciousness, and the self. The dream charts my journey from body to spirit and finally to soul, accepting my gift from the tree of life.

## PRACTICE #48

## HOW TO BRING A SOUL DREAM INTO THE BODY

When we meditate on soul dreams and bring them into our body, this helps us to focus on our higher purpose and create our own best life.

1. Meditate on your higher self as you experienced it in the dream. This could be beautiful imagery or an animal in vibrant health, or an experience such as flying joyfully or laughing with friends. It could also be powerful archetypal imagery such as a wise mentor or guide, or an experience of light.

2. Now become your higher self, or whatever in your dream feels soulful to you. This is a short, private performance. (You may want to warn family members or coworkers not to walk in on you before you get going on this!) Give yourself some space to move around. Imagine yourself becoming the wise dream fig-

ure or the stunning vista. Re-enter the sensation of being bathed in light or lifted above the world to float among the stars. Move your body if movement feels right. Sing or dance or repeat words from your dream; wave your arms in the air like tree branches or spin around in circles to embody a graceful ice skater: do whatever it takes to embody your soul dream!

3. Do this until you really feel the energy of the dream in your body. You may feel emotional or get tingling sensations. You may feel empowered.

4. Healing happens when you embody any resolved dream. If there is anything ambiguous about the imagery, remember that you can change it if you want to. Notice how your body feels when you do this. Dream bodywork can be astonishing, as the body will give you instant feedback on how your dream really feels to you. Once, I embodied a dream figure and my knees went completely wobbly. When I had mentally interacted with the dream figure and resolved the conflict in the dream, my knees were strong again. This is the litmus test of dream bodywork: you know when it has worked because you feel it *in your body*.

When you learn to embody dream images, you create a healing experience for your body, mind, and soul. The more you meditate on soul dreams, the faster you will see changes in your life as the universe accommodates and reflects this new energy you are sending out.

## How soul dreams help us to change our lives

Soul dreams can come along in our hour of need and help us to change our lives for the better. They can flag up the need for psychological change and healing or provide us with a direct experience of what we truly need in our life. When we change underlying destructive unconscious patterns, this frees us to experience something new and learn to react differently to situations.

In a book I coedited with Jean Campbell, *Sleep Monsters and Superheroes: Empowering Children through Creative Dreamplay*, Dr. David Gordon and Dani Vedros investigate the power of dreamwork with traumatized adolescents. They describe how dreams can help young offenders in correction centers, many of whom have had terribly difficult lives and have suffered abuse. They share the story of Thomas.

When he was thirteen, Thomas had his first ever experience of love and safety—in a dream.

It can be hard to imagine the lives of some deprived children who grow up with no loving physical contact, only beatings and rejection. Imagine never experiencing love or safety for the first thirteen years of life! And when it finally happens, it doesn't come from the outside world, but the inner world, in the form of a dream. No wonder Thomas behaved badly; nobody in his world had ever given him the nourishment and validation we all need. Yet dreams can help even the most disregarded of people to feel loved and valued. Through the following soul dream, Thomas began to change his inner movie, and his life improved.

---

## Thomas's dream: God Strokes My Head

*I was lying in the time-out room in my underwear. The floor was hard cement. I had never been so cold in my life. I had been fighting and acting crazy. I was so pissed off at being there I wanted to die, and I was planning to fight until I was killed or killed someone else.*

*I fell asleep on that floor and in my dream God came to me and he stroked my head and it felt really warm. I realized I was going to be OK, and that I was going to make it out of there. I kinda felt loved for the first time. He didn't say a word to me, it was just the touch.*

*I woke up crying. I wanted to live and to get out. I knew I was supposed to do something with my life, but I didn't know how or what I could do.*

When we are in need of change, soul dreams like this one come to change us. Once Thomas had the opportunity to work on his dream in a supportive, therapeutic environment, he was able to express his fears, anxiety, loss, and shame. By doing so, he changed a lifelong pattern of aggression and began to let go of his identity as a hostile victim. His soul dream became a guiding experience that he could return to whenever he needed by imaginatively re-entering the dream.

---

Soul dreams can bring us transformative spiritual experiences that inspire us to change our lives. We can recall these healing dreams in times of need to help us through life. Soul dreams help us to go beyond the external to touch the essence of ourselves. Once we recognize our essence, life becomes a million times easier, as we'll find ourselves being able to relate to others on a deeper, more honest level; soul to soul rather than body to body. We will become more authentic and discover our true purpose in life, whatever that may be.

## PRACTICE #49

### MEET YOUR SOUL

We are more than just a body and a brain: we are spirit and soul. This gentle visualization is an imaginative way of meeting your soul.

Find a relaxing, quiet space to lie down. You could record this visualization in your own voice, or ask a friend to read it slowly to you.

*Close your eyes and breathe deeply and steadily while your body relaxes.*

*Imagine you are standing on the top of a green hill in front of a beautiful temple with strong pillars and intricate carvings. Everything in this place is at the height of its beauty, and you feel a deep sense of contentment.*

*You walk towards the temple, noticing its aura of tranquillity. A wooden door stands open invitingly. As you cross the threshold and enter the temple you feel an increased sense of wellbeing and aliveness. Inside this sacred place, you look around at the warm glow of candles and feel the cool marble floor beneath your feet. Being here makes you feel as if you have finally arrived home after a long absence. This sacred place belongs to you.*

*Up ahead of you, in a broad stone circle lit with rainbow candles, you see your soul.*

*Everybody's soul looks different, but you recognize yours the moment you see it. It may appear as a pool of crystal clear water, an ancient book, a wise-eyed animal or person, a loving, compassionate light, or anything else.*

*Walk up to your soul and greet it in whatever way feels right. Then settle down and take as much time as you need to talk with it. You may want to ask it questions about your life path, or listen to an important message it has for you. Or you might simply sit beside it and experience its loving energy.*

*Finally, when you feel it's time to leave, thank your soul and take three deep breaths to bring you gently back to waking reality. Smile, open your eyes, and write about what happened, or draw it.*

Once when I did this visualization, I saw my soul as a cascading waterfall of light; taller than me, luminous, wise, and ancient. If it feels right, you can make your soul imagery part of how you see yourself, to improve your inner movie and self-esteem: "My soul is a noble stag with tree roots for antlers," or, "I am the man whose soul is a giant, healing hand."

When you have found the perfect dream imagery to depict your soul, bring your soul into your life! Use the practices in this chapter to embody this soul imagery. Remind yourself that this is who *you* are; this wise spiritual being or healing energy. Keep your soul close at all times. When you are faced with difficult situations or aggressive people, rather than buying into their drama, try to respond from the level of your soul. When you keep your soul close by keeping your dreams close, you begin to live your best life.

# Create your own best life

Now that you have worked with this book, written down your dreams, and listened to their messages, you'll know that Mindful Dreaming is about discovering that we have the power to change what we no longer need or want; both in our dreams and in our waking lives. Dreamwork is a little like magic because it allows us to dissolve the veil that covers our own hidden, unconscious world. Once the veil is gone, we can clearly see the state of our life; what it lacks and what it needs to become healthier and happier.

Whenever I am in trouble in my life, I turn to my dreams. When somebody I love dies, I seek a healing moment with them in a dream. When I get sick, I ask my dreams for help. When trauma strikes, whether I like it or not, my dreams will send me vivid pictures showing me exactly how I feel. If I need encouragement to get over something bad, they will send me nightmares until I rouse myself and deal with the issue. From a lifetime of paying attention to my dreams, I can say for sure that all dreams come to help and heal us. Even the worst nightmares.

After my baby nearly died, I was plagued by recurring nightmares in which I found her dead in her cot. For the first time in my life, I was furious with my dreaming mind—how dare it kick me when I was down! The next time the nightmare happened, I became lucid and yelled at the dream, releasing all my anger and agony. Suddenly, I felt total peace and harmony and woke buzzing with that same energy. That dream was a turning point; my anxiety levels around my baby dropped, and the healing process began.

Our dreaming mind wants us to heal. It's as simple as that, and so if we allow dreams to be our guide, they will help us do that. It's only when we heal ourselves on deep levels that we can truly help ourselves—and others—to live happier, healthier lives. By doing Mindful Dreaming for ourselves, we can help other people. When we work to heal our minds of violence, envy, fear, and hatred, we are playing our part in dreaming a happier world into existence. We are healing our collective unconscious, and from this healing a more harmonious "world dream" will emerge.

## How to create your own best life

You'll be familiar now with the way that in lucid dreams, we can observe how our thoughts, emotions, and desires impact directly on the dream environment, transforming it into whatever we are creating with our mindset. This is a fascinating lesson to teach us how our mindset affects our waking life, too.

Every thought we think and every dream we dream adds to our inner movie.

The more time we spend lucid in our dreams, guiding dream events to happier, more healing conclusions, and the more time we spend doing Lucid Dreamplay while awake, the easier it becomes to guide our waking life towards greater health and happiness. When we allow our dreams to transform in Lucid Dreamplay, we experience more positive emotions, have a deeper understanding of ourselves and others, see solutions rather than problems, develop greater empathy and compassion, and become more optimistic. We become happier. Happiness and good health go hand in hand. Scientific studies show that happiness can make our hearts healthier, our immune systems stronger, and our lives longer.

It follows that if we change our inner movie into something positive, nourishing, and supportive, we will go through life feeling positive, nourished, and supported. People around us will respond to this and our relationships will automatically grow more agreeable and mutually enjoyable. We will begin to create our own best life: the life we would love to have. If you've worked your way systematically through this book, you'll already be well on the way to creating the life you'd love to lead. This final practice sums up the main steps involved.

## PRACTICE #50

## THE FIVE-STEP PROGRAM TO CREATING YOUR BEST LIFE

1. Change the focus, scope, and potential of your inner movie through Lucid Dreamplay and lucid dreaming.
2. Recreate yourself as your best self. Allow your most positive and luminous dream imagery to remind you of your inner beauty so that you become who you want to be.
3. Auto-correct negative thoughts and scenarios. Imaginatively redirect them (as in a lucid dream) towards happier, kinder conclusions.
4. Visualize yourself living—and enjoying—your best life; the life you would love to lead. Feel gratitude for this new dream you're creating, and fully expect it to happen.
5. Absorb positive dream imagery: take time every day to breathe it into you, body and soul.

)———(

### Next steps

In this book, you have seen that once we set up a healthy sleeping routine and start keeping a dream journal, we can begin to work with our dreams in healing and empowering ways. We can transform our inner movie by doing Lucid Dreamplay, thereby changing unhelpful unconscious patterns, and we can integrate healing dream imagery into our lives. We can release fear, resolve nightmares, nurture our child self and work with dreams to ease illness and overcome loss. We can experience the vast possibilities of lucid dreaming. We have seen how to go deeper into dreams by unwrapping soul dreams, seeking spiritual experiences, and moving towards the light in dreams. We have learned how it is possible to dream ourselves well and in doing so create a happier life for ourselves.

The next steps to take are simple: keep going! Keep writing down your dreams; keep working and playing with them to increase your understanding of them and honor their message. Return to your favorite practices in the book, and try them out with new dreams. Branch out into dream art by drawing, painting, or sculpting your dreams. Dreams can provide incredible creative inspiration, and the magic never runs out, as you'll dream new dreams every single night. Have fun exploring where your dreams take you.

When you do Mindful Dreaming, you empower yourself to become your own dream therapist, and you cultivate a wonderfully rich, creative relationship with your dreaming mind.

In doing so, you lay the foundations for creating the life you would love to live.

With the help of your dreams, you can heal your life.

# RESOURCES

*The International Association for the Study of Dreams (IASD)*
For readers who would like extra care and help with their dreams or who want to deepen their exploration of dreamwork, I highly recommend becoming a member of IASD. This vibrant and friendly organization brings dreamers together from all walks of life; creates fabulous dream conferences (easy-access online ones and others in global locations); and provides a wealth of expert dream advice, insight, and information through its member-exclusive *DreamTime* magazine and its academic journal, *Dreaming*. IASD is community based, supportive, and fascinated by all aspects of dreaming. For me, it's like a second family. Find out more on *www.asdreams.org*

*The Dream Research Institute (DRI)*
Beauchamp Lodge, 2 Warwick Crescent, London W2 6NE. Phone: +44 (0)20 7266 3006. Email: *driinfo@ccpe.org.uk* Website: *www.driccpe.org.uk*
I have had the pleasure of working with DRI cofounder Melinda Ziemer in the past. The DRI offers workshops and other public events, a unique archive, teaching videos, educational courses, and therapeutic work with dreams. The DRI is part of the Center for Counselling and Psychotherapy Education (CCPE), which provides clinical services through some one

hundred practicing therapists who are also trained in working with dreams across a range of psychological issues. If you feel you could benefit from one-on-one dreamwork with a professional, see *http://ccpe.org.uk for more information.*

*Deep Lucid Dreaming*
If you're keen to learn more about the potential of lucid dreaming, on my website you can discover more about everything from lucid dream sex and creativity to how time, space, and physics work in lucid dreams. You can pick up a free e-book on how to get and stay lucid, watch video chats on different aspects of lucid dreaming, and contact me for advice or to share your most transformative experiences with Mindful Dreaming. I am occasionally available for Skype dreamwork sessions.
*www.DeepLucidDreaming.com*

# REFERENCES

p. 3 Coalson, Bob, "Nightmare Help: Treatment of Trauma Survivors with PTSD," *Psychotherapy*, 32(3), 1995, pp381–388.

p. 4 Freud, Sigmund, *The Interpretation of Dreams*, trans. James Strachey, New York, Avon Books, 1965 [1900].

p. 6 Wargo, Eric "Understanding the Have-Knots," *Observer*, Association for Psychological Science, 20(11), December 2007.

p. 7 Pert, Candace, *Molecules of Emotion: Why You Feel The Way You Feel*, New York, Scribner, 1997.

p. 7 Beth Israel Deaconess Medical Center website, "Dreams Tell Us That the Brain Is Hard At Work On Memory Functions," April 22, 2010. *http://www.bidmc.org/News/PRLandingPage/2010/April/Stickgold.aspx*

p. 8 Stickgold, Robert et al., "Sleep-Induced Changes in Associative Memory," *Journal of Cognitive Neuroscience*, 11(2), 1999, pp182–193.

p. 17 Naiman, Rubin, "The Silent Epidemic of Dream Loss," paper presented at the 15th PsiberDreaming Conference of the International Association for the Study of Dreams, September 25–October 9, 2016.

p. 21 Goodwin, Jenifer, "Sleeptime Head-Cooling Cap Eases Insomnia, Study Finds," HealthDay News, June 14, 2011. *https://consumer.healthday.com/ health-technology-information-18/research-and-development-health-news-578/ sleeptime-head-cooling-cap-eases-insomnia-study-finds-653882.html*

p. 28 Barasch, Marc, *Healing Dreams: Exploring the Dreams That Can Transform Your Life*, New York, Riverhead Books, 2000.

p. 29 Jung, C.G., *The Archetypes and the Collective Unconscious*, trans. R.F.C Hull, Collected Works 9(1), London, Routledge, 1991 [1959].

p. 44 Hearne, Keith, "Lucid Dreams: An Electro-Physiological and Psychological Study," PhD thesis, University of Liverpool, England, 1978.

p. 44  Garfield, Patricia, *Creative Dreaming*, New York, Touchstone, 1995.

p. 44  Sparrow, Scott, *Lucid Dreaming: Dawning of the Clear Light*, Virginia Beach, A.R.E. Press, 1982.

p. 44  LaBerge, Stephen, "Lucid Dreaming: An Exploratory Study of Consciousness During Sleep," PhD thesis, Stanford University, US, 1980.

p. 45  Voss, Ursula et al., "Induction of Self Awareness in Dreams Through Frontal Low Current Stimulation of Gamma Activity," *Nature Neuroscience*, 17(6), 2014, pp810–812.

p. 46  Stumbrys, Tadas, and Michael Daniels, "An Exploratory Study of Creative Problem Solving in Lucid Dreams: Preliminary Findings and Methodological Considerations," *International Journal of Dream Research*, 3(2), 2010, pp121–129.

p. 45  Johnson, Clare R., "The Role of Lucid Dreaming in the Process of Creative Writing," PhD thesis, University of Leeds, UK, 2007.

p. 47  Spoormaker, Victor, and Jan van den Bout, "Lucid Dreaming Treatment for Nightmares: A Pilot Study," *Psychotherapy and Psychosomatics*, 75(6), 2006, pp389–394.

p. 51  Schädlich, Melanie, "Darts in Lucid Dreams: A Sleep Laboratory Study," Paper presented at the 33rd Annual Conference for the International Association for the Study of Dreams, Kerkrade, The Netherlands, June 24–28, 2016.

p. 51  Erlacher, Daniel, and Michael Schredl, "Practicing a Motor Task in a Lucid Dream Enhances Subsequent Performance: A Pilot Study," *The Sport Psychologist*, 24(2), 2010, pp157–167.

p. 52  Lapina, N., V. Lysenko, and A. Burikov, "Age-Dependent Dreaming: Characteristics of Secondary School Pupils," *Sleep Supplement*, 21, 1998, pp287.

p. 77  Kiser, Barbara, "The dreamcatcher," *New Scientist*, 12 April 2003. *https://www.newscientist.com/article/mg17823904-900-the-dreamcatcher/*

p. 78  Hamilton, Nigel, "Luminescent Colors in Lucid Dreams and Visions," Paper presented at the 33rd Annual Conference of the International Association for the Study of Dreams (IASD), Kerkrade, The Netherlands, June 24–28, 2016.

p. 79  Manley, Francis, *The Effect of Intentional Dreaming on Depression*, The Fielding Institute, Santa Barbara, USA, 1982.

p. 82  Powers, Mark, and Paul Emmelkamp, "Virtual Reality Exposure Therapy for Anxiety Disorders: A Meta-Analysis," *Journal of Anxiety Disorders*, 22(3), 2008, pp561–569.

p. 83 Turner, Rebecca, "How to Cure Fears and Phobias with Lucid Dreaming." *http://www.world-of-lucid-dreaming.com/how-to-cure-fears-and-phobias-with-lucid-dreaming.html*

p. 84 Lyons, Tallulah, and Wendy Pannier, "The Healing Power of Dreams and Nightmares: The IASD Dream Work with Cancer Patients Project." *http://www.allthingshealing.com/Dream-Medicine/The-Healing-Power-of-Dreams-and-Nightmares-/3759#.WK_kjmYzVjp*

p. 86 McNamara, Patrick, "The Very, Very Strange Properties of REM Sleep," *Psychology Today*, August 13, 2011. *https://www.psychologytoday.com/blog/dream-catcher/201108/the-very-very-strange-properties-rem-sleep*

p. 90 LaBerge, Stephen, Walter Greenleaf, and Beverly Kedzierski, "Physiological Responses to Dreamed Sexual Activity During Lucid REM Sleep," *Psychophysiology* 20, 1983, pp454–55.

p. 96 Garfield, Patricia, *Pathway to Ecstasy: The Way of the Dream Mandala*, New York, Prentice Hall Press, 1979, p.140.

p. 97 Schredl, Michael et al., "Erotic Dreams and Their Relationship to Waking Life Sexuality," *Sexologies* 18(1), 2009, pp38–43.

p. 103 Freud, Sigmund, *The Interpretation of Dreams*, trans. James Strachey, New York, Avon Books, 1965 [1900].

p. 103 Schredl, Michael et al., "The Use of Dreams in Psychotherapy: A Survey of Psychotherapists in Private Practice," *The Journal of Psychotherapy Practice and Research* 9(2), 2000, p81.

p. 104 Mallon, Brenda, *Dreams, Counselling and Healing*, Dublin, Newleaf, 2000.

p. 120 Krakow, Barry et al., "Imagery Rehearsal Treatment for Chronic Nightmares," *Behaviour Research and Therapy* 33(7), 1995, pp837–843.

p. 120 Spoormaker, Victor, Jan van den Bout, and Eli J. G. Meijer, "Lucid Dreaming Treatment for Nightmares; A Series of Cases," *Dreaming* 13(3), 2003, pp181–186.

p. 124 Jung, Carl G., *Memories, Dreams, Reflections*, edited by Aniela Jaffé, New York, Random House, 1961.

p. 130 US Department of Veterans Affairs, National Center for PTSD. *http://www.ptsd.va.gov/public/problems/nightmares.asp*

p. 131 Krakow, Barry et al., "Imagery Rehearsal Treatment for Chronic Nightmares," *Behaviour Research and Therapy* 33(7), 1995, pp837–843.

p. 139 Garfield, Patricia, *The Healing Power of Dreams*, New York, Simon & Schuster, 1991.

p. 139 Mallon, Brenda, *Dreams, Counselling and Healing*, Dublin, Newleaf, 2000.

p. 140 Hartmann, Ernest, *Dreams and Nightmares: The New Theory on the Origin and Meaning of Dreams*, Pennsylvania State University, Plenum Trade, 1998.

p. 140 Burk, Larry, "Warning Dreams Preceding the Diagnosis of Breast Cancer: A Survey of the Most Important Characteristics,"*Explore: The Journal of Science and Healing*, 11(3), 2015, pp193–198.

p. 142 Banerji, Bhaskar, "Using Dreams to Elicit Inner Healing Resources: An Exploratory Study," PhD thesis, Saybrook University, US, 2017.

p. 146 Kohen, Daniel P. et al., "The Use of Relaxation-Mental Imagery (Self-Hypnosis) in the Management of 505 Pediatric Behavioral Encounters," *Journal of Developmental & Behavioral Pediatrics*, 5(1), 1984.

p. 150 Johnson, Clare R., "Amazing Dreamers: Interview with Sheila Asato," *DreamTime*, Fall 2015, pp33–34.

p. 155 Gratton, Nicole, and Séguin, Monique, *Dreams and Death: The Benefits of Dreams Before, During, and After Death*, Quebec, Flammarian, 2009.

p. 156 Hoffman, Jan, "A New Vision for Dreams of the Dying," *The New York Times*, February 2, 2016. *https://www.nytimes.com/2016/02/02/health/dreams-dying-deathbed-interpretation-delirium.html?_r=0*

p. 157 Johnson, Clare R., "Amazing Dreamers: Interview with Fariba Bogzaran," *DreamTime*, Fall 2014, pp33–34.

p. 161 Parnia, Sam et al., "AWARE—AWAreness during REsuscitation—A prospective study," *Resuscitation*, 85(12), 2014, pp1799–1805.

p. 163 Johnson, Clare R., "Amazing Dreamers: Interview with Patricia Garfield," *DreamTime*, Spring 2014, pp27–28.

p. 172 Ware, Bronnie, "Regrets of the Dying," 2009. *http://www.bronnieware.com/blog/regrets-of-the-dying*

p. 175 Jung, Carl G., *Collected Works of C. G. Jung, Volume 8: Structure & Dynamics of the Psyche*, edited and translated by Gerhard Adler and R.F.C. Hull, New Jersey, Princeton University Press, 1969.

p. 188 Gordon, David, and Dani Vedros, "The Power of Dreamwork with Traumatized Adolescents," in Clare Johnson and Jean Campbell (eds.), *Sleep Monsters and Superheroes: Empowering Children through Creative Dreamplay*, Santa Barbara, Praeger, 2016, pp123–137.

# PRACTICE LIST

# ACKNOWLEDGMENTS

This would be a lesser book without the generosity of those who were happy to share their dreams, life context, and healing process in the hope of helping others to see how transformative dreamwork can be. My heartfelt thanks!

Many thanks to my talented agent, Carrie Plitt, whose vision for a new book by me on healing dreams kick-started the process that turned into *Mindful Dreaming*. We were both delighted when the book found a wonderful home at Orion with Amanda Harris, Lucy Haenlein, and the rest of the team.

I feel very lucky to have such a supportive family who have seen me through the process of writing this book. My love and appreciation go to my husband, Markus ,and our beautiful little girl, Yazzie, who makes us laugh every day.

## TO OUR READERS

Conari Press, an imprint of Red Wheel/Weiser, publishes books on topics ranging from spirituality, personal growth, and relationships to women's issues, parenting, and social issues. Our mission is to publish quality books that will make a difference in people's lives—how we feel about ourselves and how we relate to one another. We value integrity, compassion, and receptivity, both in the books we publish and in the way we do business.

Our readers are our most important resource, and we appreciate your input, suggestions, and ideas about what you would like to see published.

Visit our website at *www.redwheelweiser.com* to learn about our upcoming books and free downloads, and be sure to go to *www.redwheelweiser.com/newsletter* to sign up for newsletters and exclusive offers.

You can also contact us at *info@rwwbooks.com.*

Conari Press
an imprint of Red Wheel/Weiser, LLC
65 Parker Street, Suite 7
Newburyport, MA 01950
*www.redwheelweiser.com*